Jean-Paul Cassone'

TANDEM

"Escape to the multipolar world"

Printed in U.S.A. for CSRV

(Cassone' Silk Road Ventures)

*(First master proofs printed at The Copy Factory, El Camino Real, Palo Alto, CA)

**(Cover art by graphic artist Bonnie B. Brewer for Compass Printing, Saranac Lake, N.Y.)

About the Author

Jean-Paul Cassone' (Italian with French pronunciation: Kass-o-nay) grew up in the then sleepy town of Bedford, New York. Historically speaking, it was burned to the ground under the British General Tarleton during the American Revolution. As irony would have it one of the author's direct descendants, James Donegan served in the British Army and was responsible for saving the life of "The Iron Duke" (The Duke of Wellington) at the Battle of Waterloo. His great grandfather, Anthony Cassone' served as a Palace Guard for the last two kings of Italy.

Two other distinctive, yet opposing branches in the author's family tree were one of the most liberal U.S. Supreme Court Justices William J. Brennan and a very conservative U.S. General Philip H. Sheridan. His grandfather Dr. Paul W. Casson was witness to a miracle in the Mother Cabrini Hospital of New York City and was summoned to testify before the Papal Court of Pope Pius VII in Rome, which later would become a deciding factor in the canonization of the first American Saint, St. Francis Xavier Cabrini.

Mr. Cassone's name was modified for 100 years to "Casson" under the Italian suffrage in New York, when the New York Railroad strictly forbid the hiring of Italians. He holds a Master's Degree in English as an Alumni of Wilmington National University and was born in Manhattan, New York and delivered by his grandfather.

His background covers a wide spectrum, first holding positions in horticulture, agriculture and sawmills for Weyerhaeuser, then in logistics and manufacturing for Pentair and Applied Materials and onto lengthy tenures in women's fashions for Polo Ralph Lauren and in printing for FedEx Office-CPC, a high security printing facility. It wasn't until he started getting a few lucky breaks overseas writing independent editorials that Jean-Paul Cassone' began building a small following. He has a reputation for being open-minded, unbiased and fair and is well liked by Chinese, Russians and Muslims, as well as Americans and Europeans.

In China the author taught intermediate English to more than 4,000 students for over 25 separate organizations and authored various articles for several news organizations in China, Iran and Pakistan.

CSRV staff writer

"The devil will lie to you twice as convincingly, than your own mother can while telling you the truth".

Jean-Paul Cassone'

(JPC-book 1)

Table of Contents

(Intentionally left blank)

Chapter One

Escape to the Multipolar World

The first impressionable occurrence of 2015 was the January 4th Full Moon. A moon which greatly motivated the Uranus-Pluto structure and Lunar Nodes, while it aligned with Sirius, a fixed star. At present astrology possess an immense energy of an eclipse which is coercing society to forge a significant opposition to widespread ferocity, gross exploitation and oppression.

Sirius and the Nodes conjure up an alluring sensation in us all that we have suddenly arrived at a fork in the road, which is telling us our choice will be irreversible.

There was a great separation this past Spring, of both worlds as they parted into two precise realities. One of horror and demise, the other of balance and brightness. Both worlds quiver at contrasting frequencies in a positive-negative divergence. And it is the degree of our self-assurance, which will decide which one of these worlds we will find ourselves in.

As both planetary formats begin to meld their circuitry to within our cosmos, we are granted a great moment to choose our mortal history. Will we desire living in an existence of caring, compassion and balance, or will we select the vindictive, cut-throat continuance of greed and exploitation? One cannot uphold the other. Let us consider for a moment the great undertow of the multipolar world. Uncoupled from our present shrinking unipolar world it shares the same orbit, but on its own, separate and slightly tilted sphere. In astronomy this is known as a "co-orbital configuration". When two co-orbital objects are of similar masses and thus exert a non-negligible influence on each other, an "exchange orbit" occurs. The objects can exchange semi-major axes, or eccentricities when they approach one another.

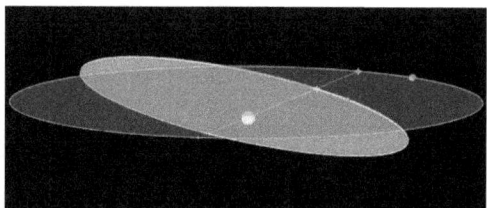

I can relate to you in more vivid detail, just exactly what series of events led up to the impetuous start of the unipolar world, later on in Chapter 3, "The Day America Died: Empires in Decline"! To make things more quickly understandable, it coincided with the date November 2, 1963, some 53 years ago and it serves as a keystone to my measurement of The American Empire of 1776 to 1963, which equals a duration of 187 years. The irony in this figure is such that not only are many Americans unaware of this fact, but that America as a nation began as a "republic" and ended as a declining empire, conquered from within.

Historians have long realized that global powers experience rhythms of growth, maturity, stability and decline. The German philosopher Hegel was aware that even though people learned about the past, it didn't guarantee them making any more sound decisions for their future. He was quoted as saying, "What experience and history teach us is this – that people and governments never have learned anything from history, or acted on principles deduced from it".

After the fall of the Soviet Union in 1991 America was elevated over the rest of the world as a towering giant. Its culture, its economics and its military were suddenly imposed and forced-fed down the throats of its neighbors, planet wide. And here we sit 25 years later, with its armed forces still battling extremists and terrorists the world over, robbing the societies of their revenues to serve its citizens and maintain good upkeep to their infrastructures. Upon a close inspection of this aspect we begin to learn that somebody or bodies within its government, has been planting, propagating and cultivating these quote, "enemies of the State" themselves.

One of the great flaws of the New World Order's unipolar intentions was "invade, divide and destroy; if no enemies come forth then hatch your own". The approach of this idiocy was to feed an ever-burgeoning Industrial Military Complex from Wall Street to the Pentagon, while leaving in its wake, an emaciated civilization.

The invasion of Libya is a case in point. Before the U.S. invaded this "democracy" it experienced the highest human development index and had the best life expectancy in all of Africa, with the lowest infant mortality rate. It possessed the best GDP per capita in Africa, had less people living below the poverty line than the Netherlands with no taxes on food and healthcare and education was "free"! Ten percent of Libyan students received foreign scholarships. The country was pumping one million, eight hundred thousand barrels of high quality oil a day and had the highest per capita income in all of the African continent. The unipolar world has clearly demonstrated that it destroys equitable distributions of geopolitical wealth which most benefits a society as a whole.

11

Italy is a simple example of how a nation and its people are being held hostage by a unipolar imposition. Being forced to impose sanctions against Russia which it clearly can't afford and doesn't agree with, it is subject to serve a role as an American aircraft carrier in the Mediterranean Sea. It is not permitted the freedom to function in connection with its natural geographical direction of the Balkans and North Africa. Only after an uncoupling from the Western tyrannical system and an orbital shift to the multipolar position, will Italy become enabled to reach its highest potential as an integral component of a free and united Europe.

Perhaps it is beginning to become clearer to you now, just how greatly the American system has changed since the loss of its functional democracy some 53 years ago. In its process of constructing a unipolar world it has designed standards which destroyed sovereignty, obliterated culture and transformed diversity into a consumerist blob of gook. In the words of Jung Xi Min, "The world is a colorful place; how sad it would be if we were all made to be the same."

The multipolar world openly permits diversity on a global scale with various groups and nations forming into many different poles, while forbidding any one group from attempting to culturally or otherwise, dominate the world. This contrasts with much brighter appeal against the many problematic aspects of the unipolar experiment, such as mass deindustrialization, death of the middle class, death of the family, death of languages and cultures, waves of mass migration, failed programs of "Tolerance" and "Political Correctness" with massive corruption, while each generation becomes poorer.

The shear irony in all of this is that what's occurring to the Western world over the decades are precisely the same things which happened to the USSR in the 1980's. The decline is clear and simple. The New World Order unipolar globalization concept is not the system which made America or Europe the envies of the world. Multipolar does = Anti-globalization.

Today America ranks 13th in starting a business, 47th in press freedoms, 20th in international trade, 15th in debt insolvency, 10th in economic freedom, 25th among 43 countries for the best place to be a mother, and 11th in happiness. There are 21 countries better than America, in freedom from corruption. Continuing, the U.S. ranked 24th in honesty, 39th in income equality, 47th in infant survival, 50th in life expectancy, 169th out of 216 countries for GDP growth, 12th in GDP per capita and worse than 102 of 200 countries for unemployment.

Here's a disgraceful one; 142nd out of 150 for infrastructure investment. In growth rate for industrial production it ranked 79th, 11th in oil exports, 192nd (dead last) in the net trade of goods and services and 79th in the amount of women holding public office.

Ready for some things this headless, unipolar behemoth is now excelling in? How about:

- #1 incarceration rate in the world

- #1 in obesity by a wide margin (no pun intended)

- #1 in divorce

- #1 for most hours daily of T.V. watched per-person-a-week

- #1 in the rate of illegal drug use

- #1 in car thefts

- #1 in rape

- #1 in murder

- #1 in total crimes

- #1 in amount of police officers

- #1 in spending on healthcare as a percentage of GDP

- #1 in the amount of people on pharmaceutical drugs

- #1 in the number of women taking anti-depressants

- #1 in student loan debt

- #1 in the amount of military bases

- #1 in most complicated tax system

- #1 in national debt with its US government debt expanding at the rate of $40,000-per-second

- #1 in pornography with 89% of the world's pornography made in the US

- #1 in trade imbalance having a negative one every year since 1976

- #1 in military spending as it spends 7x's more on the military than any other nation

Clearly America's superpower status is increasingly on the wane. While it clings to the mast of it's slowly sinking unipolar ideology it is ordained to decline and fall. Unfortunately, as you will learn further along in this book, most all of it has been purposely put into motion by its very own prestigious foundations, its central banking system and an elite criminal syndicate within its own government.

A British general and historian, Sir John Bagot Glubb (1897-1987), better known as Glubb Pasha once wrote about the collapse of great empires in his 1978 book, "The Fate of Empires and the Search for Survival". In it he describes a reoccurring pattern befitting the history of fallen empires. Glubb found that various empires had undergone the same cultural changes in a sequential order of pronounced, overlapping steps. First came 1) "the age of outburst and initial pioneering", followed by 2) "the age of conquests". Next came 3) "the age of commerce", then 4) "the age of affluence", followed by 5) "the age of intellect". And finally the last two, 6) "the age of decadence" and 7) "the age of decline".

From one progression to the next the values of people changed over time; militarily, politically, economically and religiously, these categories affected an empire's people to act and behave differently. In the first two stages the adventuresome spirt and pioneering values fuel an empire to gain power in its conquests to gain land from others. As the steps progress into the commercial and affluent stages, the businesspersons and merchants who lust in the values of material success appear to concentrate at the top of society. It should be noted that at the same time these societies downplay the value of its soldiers. According to Glubb, this was done "not from motives of conscience, but rather because of the weakening of a sense of duty in its citizenry and the increase in selfishness manifested in the desire for wealth and ease".

During this moment in an empire's evolution it ceases in taking control of more land and instead begins building walls. It is during this commercial and affluent stage which an empire switches from the offensive to the defensive. Business investment inspired by the empire's unity is what creates the wealth that elevates it to "the age of intellect". Even Genghis Khan's Mongol Empire continued supporting caravan trade throughout the renowned Eurasian Silk Road. It was during its intellect phase that the empire's leaders poured large sums of money into the establishment of educational institutions, similar to the current universities and high schools of the modern era.

As we venture further along in this intellect phase of an empire, academic scholars appear to begin gravitating towards managing schools whose curriculum is aligned with either financial success, or is just plain impractical. These schools also then start producing "skeptical intellectuals" who may oppose the beliefs and values of the empire's founding leaders. In early Rome students were offered a basic education which emphasized character development and virtue. However, later on in the Roman Empire they began teaching rhetoric and the art of speech, since passionate persuasion of assemblies began to lose their practical or political value.

The systemic effect of material wealth seems to influence both an empire's upper class and common citizens to discard the disciplinary values of self-confidence which served as the building blocks for the empire's initial creation. Decadence and a declining collapse are the last two phases which follow this point in time. As Glubb points out an empire's heroes change in sync with its values. During the last steps of an empire's duration, its people seem to think most highly of and even begin to imitate professional athletes, musicians and actors, regardless of the degree of corruption which have engulfed these final phase heroes' lives.

According to Glubb Pasha the Muslim Abbasid Empire during its 10th century Bagdad decline, saw writers complaining of the singers of love songs, claiming they were having a negative effect on its younger generation. Since people oftentimes appear to become emotionally connected to the music they love, they begin to hold their singers in higher esteem, even emulating them. Eventually its content becomes spiritually perverse, perforated with demeaning language, sexual overtones and fits of immorality and even satanic delusions which undermine their fans. Added to this is a decadent lifestyle characteristic of many musicians who practice drug abuse and promiscuous sex, inevitably impacting the society.

Glubb wrote of some key developing signs of decline such as widespread sexual immorality, the abandonment of marriage and an increasing divorce rate, all of which erode the structures of a stable family. Seneca, the first century Roman writer complained of his distaste in Rome's upper-middle class women. "They divorce to re-marry. They marry to divorce".

Many foreign immigrants often settle into an empire during its final decline which eventually spawns culture clashes and infighting. German chancellor Angela Merkel was recently reported to alluding to the fact that the efforts made to grow a multicultural society has "utterly failed" and demanded immigrants should make better attempts to incorporate themselves into society.

A third leg to a unipolar world's crumbling might be the increase of aimless pleasure-seekers and pessimistic individuals. This can be best summed up by 1 Corinthians 15:32: "Let us eat and drink, for tomorrow we die"! An aura of cynical hopelessness begins to seep throughout a declining empire at this phase. This finally takes the whole process to some final aspects of an empire being down for the count, such as extensive government assistance and funding the poor. Mark 14:7 describes it as, "Helping the poor can show Christian compassion, but such help can lead to laziness and dependency". In 2 Thessalonians 3:10-12 we get one last warning: "Such problems with the poor are especially likely when they begin to believe State-provided charity is a permanent right or entitlement".

List of empires:

	Time period	Location	Duration (yrs.)
American	1776-1963	U.S.	187
Lithuanian	1200-1569	Lithuania	369
Mayan	250-900	Central America	650
Aksumite	150-940	Ethiopia	790
Armenian	190 B.C.-428	Armenia	618
Babylonian	1900 B.C.-1600 B.C.	Mesopotamia	300
Benin	1440-1897	Nigeria	457
Bruneian	600-1888	Borneo	1,288
Byzantine	300-1453	(Greece, Anatolia, Africa, Palestine, Spain, Italy)	1,223
Carthaginian	650 B.C.-146 B.C.	North Africa	504
	Time period	**Location**	**Duration** (yrs.)
Danish	1350-1963	Denmark	600
Egyptian	1570 B.C.-1070 B.C.	Egypt	500
Ethiopian	1137-1974	Ethiopia	837
Frankish	250-950	Western Europe	700

Ghana	790-1240	(Mauritania, W. Mali)	450
Goguryeo	37 B.C.-668	(North Korea, Manchuria)	705
Gorkha	1600-1850	Nepal	474
Holy Roman	962-1806	Central Europe	844
Kanem	700-1387	Chad	687
Khmer	802-1431	Cambodia	629
Mongol	1206-1368	Mongolia	162
Pandyan	500 B.C.-1350	South India	1,850
Portuguese	1415-1999	Portugal	584
Roman	27 B.C.-476	Italy	503
Russian	1721-1917	Russia	196
Spanish	1402-1975	Iberian Peninsula	573
Third Reich	1933-1945	Germany	12
Tu'i Tonga	450-1865	Tonga	1,415
Wari	500-1100	Peru, Bolivia	600

The BRICS nations' economies are thriving. Russia, China, India, Brazil, Venezuela, Argentina and its member countries are what comprise the multipolar world and/or worlds. And it is only a matter of time and evolution before the Russian sanctions begin to be lifted from the unipolarity, outside the United States. Already Greece, Spain, Italy, Germany and even France are voicing weekly complaints that the ones which are suffering the most from this New World Order maneuver are themselves.

David Parkins

To be frank, none of these sanctioning nations ever really had their hearts in the concept, not with any degree of conviction. They are beginning to see the writing on the wall in their existence as vassal States to a fading empire (the U.S.). They also see how it's starting to lose them ever greater value and opportunities to their changing economies; far more than anything the unipolar world can offer them in return. The time is nearing for the components of the European Union to break away from the enslavement which the unipolarity of both Israel and America have been imposing upon them.

Evidence to the much greater health of the multipolar economies are listed in the following, few samples:

- Over the last 3 years China has used more cement than the United States has used in the whole 20th Century.

- The original forecast of the Indian and China economies overtaking the U.S. were pegged to the year 2060.Those figures have now been forced to be revised down to 2020, with a variable possibility of actually being overtaken by next year!

- The unipolar economies alongside them, are moving in the opposite direction.

- The combined economic output last year of the BRICS nations, nearly matched the GDP of the United States and with the U.S. being more and more known for practicing "sleazy econometrics" from the Wharton School, they likely did match or surpass them already!

The duality of the multipolar-unipolar worlds have now separated. The trend of steady growth within the BRICS nations, in tandem with the unipolar nations' trending in the opposite direction is an historic shift. This event is pulling the multipolar nations away from their old world master, whether they would like it or not. It is the cause of death itself for the New World Order while the BRICS are being pulled away from the unipolar world because they are transforming into the new masters of a not so distant tomorrow.

When hideous Western analysts begin insinuating that China's success may be nearing an end because of only a 6% growth rate, they're not stopping to realize that translates into $1 trillion. Not bad for "a bad year". At the BRICS 7th summit recently in Ufa, Russia, Russian President Vladimir Putin stated that the coming together of the BRICS, the Shanghai Cooperation Organization (SCO) and the Eurasia Economic Union (EEU) can provide a "powerful economic breakthrough". The moment is evident that the multipolar world is now in a tandem orbit all its own as it begins waltzing its way to strategic, long-term ties. The 7th BRICS summit at Ufa marks an historic milestone for it witnessed openly, the multipolar nations' conviction to shift the world's center of gravity away from the feeble old masters of the unipolar West. At its close, the New World Order was dead on arrival.

The dictionary's description of "paranoia" is as follows; "A form of mental disorder characterized by well-systemized delusions of persecution, or grandeur". This psychosis seems prevalent in the digression of Western critics, from Cheney to Brzezinski. Spouting desperate campaigns such as a lack of homogeny in the multipolar world, insinuating that racial similarity was a prerequisite to unity. They are the signs of a fading empire who is grossly mismanaging change. In this instance the wisest solutions for the unipolar world would be to rapidly shrink its dominant size around the world, both physically and militarily.

Its existence calls for a complete rebirth in the system which demands an immediate shakeout at the top, in terms of illegalities and corruption. From Tele Vi to Wall Street, to Pennsylvania Avenue, it has become a snake pit of elitist criminals. The sinking West should be "making friends", getting its fiscal house in order and confess to its mistakes and atrocities. It must seize this moment in time to honestly realize just where and how it can fit into a multipolar structure as a beneficial player of similar and "not domineering" size or demands. If the unipolar world is to survive it must surrender to change, acknowledge it, embrace it and become an equal contributor in life and not just be a taker.

In the rash out-of-touchiness of foolish paranoia, the defeated New World Order fanatics have inadvertently bestowed a "Goldilocks moment" upon the multipolar world, in their tandem orbit. The widespread, punitive and illegal economic sanctions lashed against Russia has afforded Moscow and Beijing an ideal opportunity to promote the BRICS, the SCO and the EEU as the axis of the new multipolar world. And it is the very deranged culprits who concocted the illicit schemes of economic sanctions, who are just starting to realize its mistakes.

Reality is quickly projecting glaring examples of U.S. policy going off halfcocked. Instead of partnering with Russia which would have greatly benefited the unipolar world nations from the get-go, the imposition of sanctions only gave cause for Russia to seek alternatives. This in-turn, grossly injured Europe more than anyone who already was reeling from extremely high unemployment figures. As if that wasn't suicidal enough, the U.S. and Israel began incubating their own strains of terrorist extremists in Syria which in turn sent a tsunami of refugees into the EU and the outcome will be horrid. History has repeatedly proven that when you mix mass immigration with high unemployment you get an explosion of civil unrest. Soon Italy, Greece, Spain and Germany will be forced to drop all sanctions, in order to gain control over their societies and economies. The remainder of Europe will follow and the U.S. will become a very lonely place.

The BRICS now have a solution to America's loan sharks, the World Bank and the International Monetary Fund (IMF). Both entities have also been the cause for the economic enslavement of many developing countries in the past. The BRICS' New

Development Bank (NDB) is now the multipolar world nations' fresh and more flexible alternative, which just held its first board meeting and will begin lending internationally.

All BRICS nations are members in China's Asia Infrastructure Investment Bank (AIIB). This organization, along with the NDB, will destroy the monopoly of the World Bank and the IMF while likely causing them to become more transparent. An official from China's Global Times stated, "It will motivate the World Bank and the IMF to function more normally, democratically and efficiently, in order to promote the reform of an international financial system, as well as the democratization of international relations". A new international framework is taking shape. In the past American and British intelligence agents implanted themselves within the World Bank and IMF as "consultants". They were responsible for sabotaging the economies of free-minded, developing nations, assassinating nationalist leaders and honest bureaucrats and generally becoming "economic terrorists"; part of the same, anti-democratic machinery which took control of the U.S., after the Kennedy assassination coup of 1963.

The New Development Bank will begin with total funds of $50 billion, which will be increased to $100 billion in two years. It is headed by India's eminent banker K.V. Kamath, former Chairmen of India's largest private sector bank ICIC, who is also the Chairman of the IT bellwether Infosys. NDB will serve as a perfect fit for the likes of large Russian enterprises such as Rosneft, Novatek and Sberbank. The corporations otherwise would have been impacted by the West's rash judgements in using sanctions.

The perception of the world is quite drastically changing. Western sanctions now have put Washington on the defensive, being exposed for criminal actions as it has committed in Ukraine, Mali, Libya, Syria and the Middle East, while creating a mass migration crisis in Germany and the greater parts of the EU. Russia's President Vladimir Putin has demonstrated a remarkable and historic nobility to peace through his exercising of great restraint against a backdrop of a demented West. The top 1% of the unipolar universe now consists of financial terrorists, psychopaths, Zionist-Jewish racists and an Israeli-Washington crime syndicate cabal, if you will. This Dr. Evil's circus on steroids comes complete with military protection of heroin from Afghanistan to Ohio, the human trafficking of hundreds of thousands of Eastern European women for an Israeli sex slave underworld, while its Washington politicians are paid-off in above-the-law, insider trading scams wherein even its Federal Reserve Board members and U.S. Treasury officials play an active role. A mandatory "random drug-testing program" of all U.S. House and Senate members would likely cause a major filibuster in this day and age as cocaine abuse has now been reported to be yet another toxic element to this embarrassing excuse for a government.

In the careful navigation of the multipolar world to steer clear of Washington psychotics, some of whom still lust for a nuclear war, Russian President Vladimir Putin utilized an astounding example of how to manage change which was brought to the forefront in crystal clear focus. He first began to remind and teach the West what the international law behind the United Nations' Charter declares, as well as how Russia is infinitely following the Charter in its conduct, especially in Syria.

It must be realized that it was Russia, not the U.S., who was formally requested by the legitimate government of Syria for support in eradicating terrorism. President Assad was democratically and fairly elected to a second term in office by the Syrian people. What the West is failing to do is to stop behaving as the world's enemy. Its antics have gotten so outlandish it often portrays itself as even being the enemy of its own people. As a case in point that its integrity has completely evaporated, it has been proven it was Turkish-U.S.-Israeli operatives who gassed-to-death Syrian victims, not Assad. Seriously, the extremes to which the West has extended itself are clearly becoming something straight out of "Dr. Strangelove".

President Putin clearly set truth free at the unipolar world's Washington and NATO leadership. On the topic of national sovereignty he asked, "What is the meaning of State sovereignty, the term which has been mentioned by our colleagues here? It basically means freedom, for every person and every State being free to choose their future. By the way, this brings us to the issue of the so-called legitimacy of the State authorities. You shouldn't play with words and manipulate them. In international law, international affairs, every term has to be clearly defined, transparent and interpreted the same way by one and all."

The President continued, "We are all different and we should respect that. Nations shouldn't be forced to all conform to the same development model that somebody has declared the only appropriate one. We should all remember the lessons of the past. For example, we remember from our Soviet past, when the Soviet Union exported social experiments, pushing for changes in other countries, for ideological reasons and this often led to tragic consequences and caused degradation instead of progress".

Those glaring words manifested precisely what is wrong in the defective international order of today. In the words of F. William Engdahl, "Nations above all, the one proclaiming herself Sole Superpower, Infallible Hegemon, the U.S.A., has arrogantly moved after the collapse of the main adversary, the Soviet Union in 1990, to create what can only be called a global totalitarian empire, what G.H.W. Bush, in his September 11, 1991 address to Congress called "a New World Order".

President Putin stated further, "Instead of learning from other people's mistakes, some prefer to repeat them and continue to export revolutions, only now these are 'democratic' revolutions. Just look at the situation in the Middle East and Northern Africa..., problems have been piling up a long time in this region and people there wanted change. But what was the actual outcome? Instead of bringing about reforms, aggressive intervention rashly destroyed government institutions and the local way of life. Instead of democracy and progress there is now violence, poverty, social disasters and total disregard for human rights, including even the right to life".

Putin addressed the U.S. and NATO role in creating ISIS; "..., the Islamic State itself did not come out of nowhere. It was initially developed as a weapon against undesirable, secular regimes. Having established controls of Syria and Iraq, the Islamic State now aggressively expands into other regions. It seeks dominance in the Muslim world and beyond.....,. The situation is extremely dangerous. In the circumstances it is hypocritical and irresponsible to make declarations about the threat of terrorism and at the same time, turn a blind eye to the channels used to finance and support terrorists, including revenues from drug trafficking, the illegal oil trade and the arms trade".

Washington has suddenly found itself grossly exposed to the eyes of the world in backing terrorists against a "democratically" elected State leader and government in Syria. Now other nations, even EU members are beginning to ask questions like this: "How is it that the U.S. with over 6,000 airstrikes in more than a year, has permitted the ISIS stronghold to only expand, while in just 72 hours the Russian Air Force destroyed more than 50 ISIS targets, brought the ISIS combatants to a shear panic and caused more than 600 of them to immediately desert and disband? There is no other excuse than to accuse some within the U.S. Industrial Military Complex of 'intentionally' instructing U.S. pilots to bomb off-target and/or 'dead targets' in order to render the appearance of engagement. In actuality this bilked the American taxpayers to line elitists' pockets, while permitting ISIS to further its course. This is the conduct of a falling empire"!

Now with more truths exposed, Washington has been seen by all as playing a very dirty double game. Germany and other EU member nations are starting to agree with admission, that President Putin has demonstrated that Russia is truly the most vital component to the urgent needs of a peace process in the Syrian war.

To trace things back to their origins many might wonder just how and where this harebrained, unipolar idea first got its traction. The Project for the New American Century (PNAC) might be considered a major incubator of the New World Order's shenanigans, at least in terms of it gaining political grip during present times. It was a neoconservative think tank based in Washington D.C., which focused on foreign policy. First being established in 1997, it was a non-profit educational organization founded by William Kristol and Robert Kagan. Its basic objective was the promotion of American global leadership. The PNAC proclaimed that "American leadership was good for both America and for the world" and they attempted to gain backing for a policy of military might and moral focus.

From the twenty-five people who signed the organization's founding principles, ten went on to serve in the G.W. Bush administration which included Dick Cheney, Donald Rumsfeld and Paul Wolfowitz. Observers Irwin Stelzen and David Grondin have commented that the Project for a New American Century played a major role in forming policy of the Bush administration, especially in drawing support for the Iraq War. Two points that are food for further thought are one, what role did Zbigniew Brzezinski serve in all of this and two, the PNAC's initial start also led up to "The 9-11 Incident".

PROJECT FOR THE NEW AMERICAN CENTURY
I guess now it's pretty clear just what that
"project" was

Steering clear of conspiracy theorists, it is public knowledge today that at least one of these geopolitical clubs' members (Dick Cheney), along with the Mossad (Israeli intelligence / Israel's CIA), both condoned and felt a need for a staged "Pearl Harbor-like event" in furthering the PNAC's major objectives. Just think about that a minute. The Project for a New American Century and Israel's Central Intelligence Agency agreed that killing 3,000 Americans on national T.V. was a reasonable means to justify its' ends! One can only guess that at this juncture in time (2001) is when the psychopaths starting winning all the PNAC's votes and "leadership" and "moral focus" were suddenly tossed out with the baby and the bath water.

It should also be mentioned that it is now both public, "proven" knowledge that the Iraq War was planned many years in advance with the intent to take down seven governments in five years.

The PNAC shut-down in 2006 and was then replaced by a new think tank, The Foreign Policy Initiative. This also shared the same founders Kristol and Kagan. Mr. Kristol, a well-known Zionist who often prefers putting Israel's interests before America's, was often seen having Republican presidential candidate Marco Rubio on a tight leash. Kristol demonstrates no tolerance for multipolar thinking and along with the company he keeps, vehemently hates Russia and Vladimir Putin. I can only offer an organization which preaches a foreign policy of hate and war, definitely doesn't have your best interests in mind.

The Foreign policy Initiative (FPI) and what it proclaims to stand for, might be difficult for some to swallow, given their support for what's happened in Palestine, Egypt, Afghanistan, Libya, the Ukraine and now Syria, since its inception. Their website lists that the FPI is devoted to actively supporting democratic allies, human rights and a strong military ready to meet the challenges of the 21st Century and strengthening America's global economic competitiveness. It was founded in 2009 and is led by Executive Christopher J. Griffin. The Foreign Policy Initiatives' Board of Directors are former Undersecretary of Defense for Policy, Eric Edelman, Dan Senor, William Kristol and Robert Kagan.

As with the PNAC, the FPI's proclaimed ideals always appear to run counter to their supported means. They mention the "rising and resurgent powers of China and Russia" as if the U.S. is saying, "it's our way, or no way and I am your boss", in a childish, sandbox manner of speaking. They talk of "other autocracies that violate the rights of their citizens", yet mention nothing concerning the abundant human rights violations of their own, both at home and abroad.

The FPI mentions "rogue states" and "Al Qaeda" sponsored terrorism, then openly condones supporting what they claim to oppose. They further claim the FPI opposes States which serve as havens for criminals, shortly after a Wikileaks released U.S. Intelligence study had issued a paper titled; "Israel, Land of Organized Crime", which had discovered hundreds of thousands of Eastern European women being smuggled and processed as sex-slaves. The U.S. and "the glorious FPI" haven't lifted a finger to save these helpless victims. You may search YouTube for David Duke + Israel Land of organized crime, for a full length video narrative.

In observing the unipolar think tanks (or Kristol Clubs) of a New World Order mindset, one quickly notices a pattern in which all the so-called "evil acts" being done in the world which they proclaim to oppose, actually correlates into "oh no, these types of methods are only reserved for us"! This bad habit of the unipolar mindset to constantly say one thing then do the opposite finally came to a head last July, 2014. The Washington Post reported from a Reuters' copy of a President Obama speech: "..., part of people's concern is just the sense that around the world the old order isn't holding and we're not quite yet to where we need to be, in terms of a new order....,".

And finally therein lies the answer to the riddle of the failed, New World Order. It never stood for "order" at all, only "disorder". This is evident in everything it touches. They destroy and break anything that used to work for people, even democracies, then leave it decimated in ruins and chaos. Not exactly trendy geopolitics.

In 2015, "Spirit Science" listed "25 Signs the Global Elites' Plan is Failing", by Lance Schuttler:

1: Fifty-seven nations were approved as founding members of the China-led Asia Infrastructure Investment Bank. Notable countries who signed on June 29th, 2015 included Russia, India, Iran, Switzerland, Germany, France, Saudi Arabia, Australia, Indonesia, the U.K., Italy and Austria. Notables who did not join: the U.S. and Japan.

2: Russia asks Greece to join the BRICS Alliance.

3: The Pentagon released documents to Judicial Watch, a government watchdog law firm, proving that the U.S. Government played a central role in creating ISIL. Interestingly, the mainstream media failed to cover this story. A few weeks later, former U.S. Intelligence officials confirmed the report.

4: Greece's Prime Minister Alex Tsipras, writes an open letter warning European leaders they are "making a grave mistake" and suggests they re-read Hemingway's "For Whom the Bell Tolls".

5: The U.S. Federal Government was hacked as the personal data of 4 million current, former and prospective employees believed to have been breached. Three weeks later F.B.I. Director James Comey, told U.S. senators the actual number could be 18 million. Some believe the hack was coordinated to gather further evidence of crimes by certain government officials.

6: Kentucky Senator Rand Paul calls for the U.S. Government to declassify 28 pages in the 9-11 attack report, which the Bush Administration blacked out.

7: Famous musician Akon announces his Solar Academy will bring solar power to more than 600 million people in Africa.

8: Whistle-blower Edward Snowden says a "profound difference" had occurred, since releasing the NSA documents and that the balance of power has shifted in our world.

9: "There will be a reset of the financial industry". The International Monetary fund says that the Chinese yuan is no longer undervalued. This sets the stage for the yuan to be recognized as the global reserve currency, something the U.S. dollar (backed by oil and war) does not like.

10: Deutsche Bank, one of the world's largest banks see's co-CEO's Jain and Fitschen resign. Two days later, German prosecutors raided the bank's headquarters in a criminal tax-fraud probe.

11: China says the G-7 Summit in Germany was "a gathering of debtors".

12: J.P. Morgan's number 2, the Vice Chairman Jimmy Lee, suddenly dies. Since 2013, 70 high-level banking officials have died, many unexpectedly.

13: Russia and China announce that all natural gas and crude oil sales, between the two countries, will be settled in Chinese yuan and converted to Rubles.

14: The State of Texas has signed a bill calling for the repatriation of its gold, from the U.S. Federal Government.

15: The Greece Parliament's Debt Committee released a report that the debt Greece owes is illegal, illegitimate and odious, according to international law. They further stated, the IMF and the European Central Bank have illegally and knowingly imposed these debts upon Greece and other nations.

16: Baron David de Rothschild is indicted by a French court for financial fraud. French Police have been ordered to track him down.

17: In a 2-1 ruling by the 2nd U.S. Circuit Court of Appeals, Bush era officials can be held liable for detaining innocent people after the 9-11 attack.

18: While European leaders try to save face on the debt crisis, Greek Prime Minister Alexis Tsipras was in Russia and gave a speech at the St. Petersburg Economic Forum. He stated that the economic center has already shifted. Greece and Russia then signed a 2 billion ruble gas pipeline deal.

19: Greece votes "NO" to the creditors' bailout offer.

20: The BRICS Bank officially opens.

21: The New York Stock Exchange was taken down for several hours and The Wall Street Journal was taken off-line, shortly thereafter. United Airlines was forced to ground all its flights, due to computer issues and 2,500 people lost power in Washington D.C.

22: One David Wilcock announces that Anonymous is working with certain U.S. military personnel to legally takedown the banking elite.

23: Iran, China, Russia, France, Germany, the U.K. and U.S. reach an historic deal on Iran's nuclear program. Its greatest opponents were Israel, Benjamin Nctanyahu, the Bushes, Marco Rubio and Ted Cruz. *(Rubio and Cruz are both William Kristol lapdogs).

24: Santa Cruz County votes to stop doing business with J.P. Morgan, Chase, Barclays, Citigroup, Royal Bank of Scotland and UBS.

25: The author-source of these 24 listings (Lance Schuttler) asks that you share them with friends. He also recommends the reader look into former Asian Pacific Bureau Chief for Forbes, Benjamin Fulford (who reported #21 and #22). He also suggests Neil Keenan, who claims to be working with well-connected sources to open up "the Global Collateral Accounts". Keenan insists these accounts were somehow tied to the JFK assassination and that the banking elite does not want the public to learn of their existence.

The acronym BRIC refers to the countries Brazil, Russia, India and China. It was first coined in 2001 by Jim O'Neill of Goldman Sachs, in a paper entitled, "Building Better Global Economic BRICs". The acronym has come into widespread use to symbolize the shift in global economic power away from the G-7's unipolarity.

In 2010 the BRICs accounted for more than 25% of the world's land area and more than 40% of the world's population. At that time they also represented 25% of the world's gross income. Their combined GDP is $20 trillion. The BRICS four leading countries already have, or are seeking an escape towards its multipolar membership. Jim O'Neill, the global economist for Goldman Sachs states that, "the economic potential of Brazil, Russia, India and China could become the four most dominant economies by mid-century". Reflected in O'Neill's thesis is the forecast predicting that China and India will become the leading suppliers, while Brazil and Russia are expected to lead in raw materials. Of the entire four, Brazil remains the only one with the capacity to continue the full spread of elements, manufacturing, services and resources, all at the same time.

Tushar Poddar and Eva Yi compiled a report which informs us that India has 10 of the world's 30 fastest-growing urban areas. Based on current trends they expect a mind-boggling 700 million people to move to the cities by mid-century. The implications of the demands this will impose upon urban infrastructure, real estate and services is significant. By all likely accounts from numerous statistical data, China seems poised to pass the U.S. in equity market capitalization, plus match America's GDP, both in less than 5 years. From a Forbes report just a few years ago the BRICS countries counted 301 billionaires, exceeding the number in Europe of 300. Brazil's economy recently passed the U.K.'s, while China became the world's largest trading country, as of 2013.

Brazil is 3rd in renewable energy and 4th in both the number of mobile phones and road networks. Brazil's lower growth rate obscures the fact that the country is wealthier than China or India on a per-capita basis, has a more developed and global financial system and has an economy potentially more diverse than its BRICS siblings, due to its raw materials and manufacturing capabilities. Russia is #1 in land mass and #3 in electricity consumption, military expenditures and rail networks. Its declining population is forecast to stabilize and grow by 2020 and has already actually met that forecast at the end of this past 2015. India is #2 in population, number of mobile phones, number of internet users, active troops and road networks. It is #3 in GDP and U.N. peacekeepers and #4 in electricity consumption.

And finally, China. China is #1 in population, labor force, exports, foreign exchange reserves, electricity consumption, renewable energy, number of mobile phones used, and number of internet users, motor vehicle production and active troops. It is 2nd in GDP, imports, current account balances, military expenditures and rail networks. China stands at 33 in area of land mass and road networks and is #4 in received FDI's.

It should be noted that all these countries hold some of the world's largest gold reserves, which shall enable them to survive well through the coming 2016-2017 crisis. The U.S. possesses next to none.

From 2020 to 2050 nine of the ten largest countries by incremental GDP are occupied by BRICS and N11 nations. The MIKT was another acronym created by O'Neill, which stands for Mexico, Indonesia, South Korea and Turkey. However, that meaning is in the midst of disintegrating as more than half of those nations are seeking possible BRICS memberships, while Turkey has been removed from everyone's equation, since the misfortunate exposure of its president and his family's support of ISIS and additional criminality. There have also been other concepts of new polarities in development such as CIVET, standing for Columbia, Indonesia, Vietnam, Egypt and Turkey. Imagine if you will, as many as 4 to 9 separate multipolar worlds (almost a mimicking of the number of planets), all sharing the same orbital path, tilted at varying degrees, crossing path intersections at alternate intervals. This is the most popular and preferred way of economic and geopolitical thinking taking shape in our galaxy today. It is proving to offer all nations the best free systems to grow at their own will and pace, while partnering with others who are similar to their location, region, size, needs and habits. Multipolarity enables nations, no matter how small, the ability to gain much greater leverage, while freeing themselves from the Western loan sharks and Zionist exploitations, not to mention the handicaps of military impositions.

And the longer Western nations continue living in their own fantasies instead of adapting to and managing change, the ever further their orbital paths will begin to drift away in distance from all global prosperity, towards the outskirts of global civilization and into the darkness of a cold alienation.

Once again America's neocons and extremists are fleecing its citizenry by navigating their nation's policies in the complete opposite direction of prosperity and global consensus. Perhaps there needs to be a DNA study of these individuals? After all, these unipolar fanatics all seem to share the same, highly negative traits: hate, possessed with control, destroying self-identity, sovereignty, culture, racial and sexual differences, freedom, happiness, a middle class and a greater sharing of wealth distribution. Basically the West's neocons and liberal extremists all share the same habits of unnecessary and manufactured wars, never sharing anything good, never attaining the point known as "enough" and appear consistently unable to experience any sense of "contentment", balance, harmony, respect and peace. They are parasitic to the blood of all unlike them and it is high time they be reclassified as "the most serve variety of terror" and be tried as the relentless destroyers of humankind that they actually are!

It has been said that WWIII has already begun. In their usual, vulgar manner, America's extremist ideologs helped orchestrate the coup in Ukraine and the destabilization of Chechnya, Belorussia, or Georgia. In their attempts to switch Russia's neighbors to the dark side they also included Tibet and Hong Kong to simultaneously destabilize China.

Beyond those maneuvers, a more quiet and lethal attack was transpiring. To destroy the Russian economy in the hopes of causing a hungry population which would make things much easier for them to manipulate. Governments who are made to be on the verge of bankruptcy, get stripped of their negotiating abilities. "These are America's terrorists"; they conduct themselves as terrorists whether it's financial or economic, so why shouldn't the rest of the world start to refer to them for what they actually are! America's terrorists' first measure was imposing sanctions against Russia. Soon after this the price of oil magically dropped from $100 a barrel to near $60. At this point we know that the markets are being seriously manipulated. This was a deliberate political move, not to mention highly illegal.

Now the U.S. also produces oil and its fracking technology is expensive to operate, requiring more than $80 a barrel to sustain profitability. The fracking business was one of the main recipients of loans ($550 billion to be exact) during the recent money creation frenzy. By illegally permitting the American terrorists to rig markets for geopolitical gain is a travesty to justice and purely "financial terrorism". It will cause a coming wave of defaults in the oil industry and have vast consequences for the entire banking system. It is currently being estimated that $220 to $260 "trillion" in toxic derivatives are currently now circulating through the global economic system, hatched by these individuals.

As if this wasn't enough felonious acts for Zionist America's terrorists, they continued their malicious crime spree by attacking the ruble, in the hopes of destroying the Russian currency. Was this more of those virtuous proclamations inspired by The Foreign Policy Initiative? For a few months thereafter the ruble began slowly eroding against the dollar. Now Russia was criminally being forced onto the ropes with dropping oil prices, like getting mugged in a gas station. An orchestrated, speculative attack began against the ruble on December 17th, 2014. Transaction volumes were gushing, with the majority being placed from London.

Two main tactics were used:

1: Borrowing rubles to sell and buy dollars.

2: Short-selling of the ruble into a wind of massive selling. After two days of these devious shenanigans the ruble fell from 58 to 75, then went back to its original level and stabilized. This speculative raid by Western financial terrorists ended in utter failure. Russia was quick to raise its interest rates to 17%, making things very expensive to buy rubles. Russia and China then sold massive amounts of dollars and bought rubles at abnormally cheap prices. By the end of the game Russia and China made off with handsome profits, leaving the American terrorists the losers.

The BRICS nations are keenly familiar with the unethical practices of the West's "new", not-so-free, rigged market antics. For decades they've been patiently and methodically moving to achieve a complete freedom from their imprisonment to the U.S. dollar (USD). They've become ever savvy in creating various de-dollarization solutions. This has allowed many more currency swaps, stocks, bonds, development banks, oil and gas, industrial equipment and bilateral trades and transactions to be executed in local currencies and maneuver away from US dollar requirements.

Russia and China are also accelerating their reductions of dollar reserves. During September of 2013 China announced it would stop stockpiling dollars. It was the main holder of dollars in the world and de-dollarization campaigns are causing a notable effect. Petrodollar exports were negative in 2014 for the first time since 1997.

In this worldly chess game President Putin of Russia and his Chinese counterpart have executed astute master moves using manipulations from the West's financial terrorists against them. Case in point, they have taken full advantage of the overvalued dollars and the undervalued prices of gold. We're talking some incredibly large volumes. China is not only the largest producer of gold in the world, but the largest importer as well. For just 2013 alone it produced 400 tons while importing another 1,200 tons. Since 2000 they've accumulated some 6,000 tons and those figures will rise much higher before the end of this year.

China's gold import hub is in The Shanghai Gold Exchange Vault, where gold withdrawals can amount to exceeding 50 tons-a-week, repeatedly surpassing the world's production. Russia is also on track just as handsomely. It is the #3 producer of gold in the world and will soon be #2. Since 2008 Russia's gold reserves have increased 160%. At the present pace the physical gold purchases of Russia and China combined would equal some 10,000 tons-a-year. This is 3 x's the world's annual production. The U.S. gold reserves are gone. With the dollar markets now posed to crash and gold reserves positioned to skyrocket, one can say with confidence that Russia and China are in perfect pitch with market forces as they sit atop the most secure economies on the planet.

President Vladimir Putin's geopolitical policies are based on the respect for sovereign nations, cooperation and the emergence of a truly multipolar world. The U.S. Empire is no different than those of the past. It always needs more money, natural resources and slaves to keep itself afloat. In contrast, the dawning of an alternative world or worlds intimidates the U.S. monopoly on those assets. As a result the BRICS have become the prime enemies of a U.S. Empire who cannot tolerate any competitor, economically, financially, politically, militarily, or ideologically. In their minds the old New

World Order types are staggering around in an undeclared world war, pulling levers and pushing buttons at random.

A vigilant reminder should be made here. As you recall the lessons which we learned in the underpinnings of Kristol and Kagan's two organizations, The Project for a New American Century and The Foreign Policy Initiative. For more than 200 years a law abiding U.S. citizen could not be taken into custody without due process and the right to legal counsel. But now you must never forget the double-speak and reverse thought process of these American terrorists. They invented and created "terrorism", dating back to before the infamous "Levon Affair". They did this in a deliberate attempt to gain control over all people. Today, under their new laws and the removal of rights, all one government official has to do is put the "t" word (terrorist) into your profile and you can legally be abducted, "privately" tried, tortured and hung or shot-to-death without a phone call, the right to an attorney, or a public jury selection. By changing free markets to their riggings they have disguised their misdeeds and illegalities.

Simultaneously, they are herding evermore numbers of Americans onto various dole programs such as food stamps, to create a reliance on the State. With historic approval ratings of Washington officials coming in as low as 10% or less, it sets off a glaring red alert in this so-called "democracy". The systematic practices of America's political terrorists have "imposed" their ideologies upon its citizens, the very people they're supposed to represent in delegating "the people's consensus". In a growing conversion from "representation" to "imposition" and the curtailment of rights into no rights and prosperity into austere dependence, the U.S. has reset its polarity towards a more Totalitarian Statehood. America's political terrorists have anointed themselves the exclusive rights to control the world, all peoples (including their own), all wealth and all things. President John F. Kennedy was cut from a cloth which believed that God was always greater than humankind. These people are operating from the standpoint that they are God. Through blackmail, extortion, pay-offs, bribes, sex, drugs and mind-control, they have traduced and sedated American's representation in the deceptive desolation of a unipolar, prison nation.

Dr. Paul Craig Roberts, former Assistant Treasury Secretary under Reagan and the brainchild of "Reaganomics" posted one of many of his continuing, insightful comments on "The 4th Media" website titled, "A Decisive Shift in the Power Balance Has Occurred and the World Knows it". In it he explains that the world is beginning to realize that a sea of change in world affairs occurred on September 28, 2015 when President Vladimir Putin of Russia stated in his U.N. speech that Russia can no longer tolerate Washington's vicious, stupid and failed policies, which have unleashed chaos that is engulfing the Middle East and now Europe. Syrian President Assad has since commented, "The West cries for refugees with one eye, while aiming a gun with the other".

Two days later Russia took ownership of the war against terrorism and in just 72 hours, accomplished tenfold what the West had failed to attain in the previous sixteen months. Sputnik news reports that some of Obama's high-security advisors had suggested he remove U.S. military forces from Syria and stand-down any intentions of overthrowing the country's "two-term", democratically elected president. They urged Obama to seek cooperation with Russia to help stop the refugee exodus which was hemorrhaging Washington's slave States in Europe. Several commentators such as Mike Whitney and Stephen Lendman expressed there is nothing Washington can do as it related to Russian actions against the Islamic State. Whether the same Israeli-U.S. gang, which concocted "The 9-11 Incident" were responsible for the downing of the Russian airliner, I cannot yet gain enough physical evidence, even though it bears questioning. America's political terrorists have now become infamous for "false-flag" attacks, so much so that the majority of the free world now immediately makes the associations. Someday America's pranksters will find themselves being "the boy that cried wolf" as their words no longer carry any credibility and they are now the nation who is bankrupt.

Dr. Roberts's brilliance concluded, "Washington's response consists of name-calling, bluster and more lies, some of which are echoed by its evermore doubtful vassals. The only effect is to demonstrate Washington's impotence. If Obama had any sense, he would dismiss from his government the neoconservative morons who have squandered Washington's power and focus instead on holding onto Europe by working with Russia to "destroy" rather than "sponsor" the terrorism in the Middle East, which has overwhelmed Europe with refugees. If Obama cannot admit a mistake, the United States will continue to lose credibility and prestige around the world".

Widespread panic set-in at the Pentagon, White House and NATO, as a modest Russian air campaign was launched in Syria. Russia's advanced air and sea power successfully destroyed 40% of the terrorist infrastructure in just one week. This also reveals an ugly truth. Many policy critics and military analysts from around the world are now deducting that the U.S. Industrial Military Complex has been fleecing American taxpayers by staging over 6,000 sorties in Syria which seemed to have purposely landed on false or dud targets.

As the world watches this unfold, it becomes evident that the U.S. coalition, with its vast airpower and resources, was no longer capable of doing what the Russians had accomplished. The padding of U.S. military funding, purely for the gain of a few Washington insiders was now exposed to both the taxpayers and embarrassingly the entire free world. The "anti-Russian media campaign" of the West has failed in amateur fashion. The world has suddenly awakened to the fact that the same pathetic souls who were a part of this campaign, also brought us 250,000 dead in Syria alone; not many of them "terrorists"!

Maram Susli is an activist-journalist and social commentator, covering Syria and geopolitics, as well as for the online magazine "New Eastern Outlook". She has accumulated a remarkable motherlode of insightful, unbiased facts. For example the former U.S. Defense Intelligence Agency Chief (DIA) Michael Flynn commented in an interview, that he believed the U.S. had made a willful decision to allow ISIS to grow. It has become increasingly clear that the U.S.'s main objective was not their expressed goal of "fighting ISIS". And the New World Disorder saga, like a bull in a China shop, continues...,.

The U.S. political terrorists within its government body have repeatedly refused to work with Syria militarily which is commanded by a U.N.-recognized government. These ridiculous extremists, be they neoconservative, or the Bilderberg Group's Hillary Clinton have attempted to repeat Libya on a grander scale by shunning a two-term, democratically elected President of Syria, so they could successfully destabilize, destroy and control everything that currently functions properly, or that benefits the people of Syria. Renowned author and lecturer David Icke had recently posted his interpretation of this, to his website, "The ISIS Technique. Train them, fund them, arm them, then kill them, but not too many".

Denial, ignorance and highly corrupt arms dealing has all been shown to the light by the U.S.'s recent stance in the Middle East. The irony which arises from Russia's valuable and intelligent, strategic conduct in Syria baffles the mind. Rather than seize this valuable opportunity to achieve peace for all by developing a precious partnership with Syria and Russia, the U.S. has chosen to throw infuriated convulsions of anger at Russia's bombing of Al Qaeda targets. By refusing to confess to the truth that "moderate rebels" is a misnomer, is in and of itself a global embarrassment. What the American public needs to wake up to, is the pure and simple fact that if these "extremist think tanks" and "corrupt policy makers" in their government are not soon apprehended and booted out of the Washington loop, both Israel and the United States can soon be legally classified as "terrorist States" promoting State sponsored terrorism which is legitimate grounds for the remaining free world to attack and destroy us as the true world's enemy. The war on terror is a fraud. A fraud to gain control over you; that and to gobble up oil for oligarchs while causing the devastation of all in its wake. It is not fighting terrorism, because it is terrorism.

When it came time to bailout the West's too big to fail banks, if those funds had been instead, equally divided amongst every man, woman and child in America, each would have received $40,000 apiece. The West has made complete buffoons of themselves by installing bank robbers in charge of the banks and terrorists in charge of their foreign policies.

And just when you thought we had successfully isolated all of the West's major fruitcakes, the Duke of Edinburgh's Prince Philip decided to bestow some of his lovely words of wisdom upon us: "If I were to be reincarnated, I would wish to be returned to Earth as a killer virus, to lower the world's human population levels". Obviously my theory on regulated breeding holds true; being thoroughly bred does produce insanity!

As the world's population approaches 6.5 billion people, let us first take a look at the many good people who have already died before a completed life. Four million were slaughtered in the Congo, two million (mostly children) were killed in Iraq wars and on average the 21st century has been churning out about 7 Jewish holocausts-a-year. Thus far we have covered in this chapter the internal changes within empires and the alternate polarities which they spawned. We also explored economic and geopolitical forces which constantly swirl in the undercurrents, giving challenge to their capabilities and eventual achievements. We have gained a clearer focus of who its real heroes and villains are, as we were afforded a greater awareness of the present day unipolarity's underpinnings and its key culprits who keep bringing forth ever greater amounts of wastefulness and destruction, which finally gave birth to the multipolar alternative.

Towards the latter part of the United States duration as a democracy (1776-1963), both Presidents Eisenhower and Kennedy forewarned Americans of the dangerous possibilities in permitting an Industrial Military Complex to grow and interlock with Wall Street. Today there is yet a new, great monster of comparable size and scope, the "Sustainable Climate Change Complex". It's nice to be conscientious and kind to the environment, but be forewarned the duality of perception will play tricks on you, should you permit yourself in getting too tangled up in the allure of this beast.

Freelance scientist-physicist James Lovelock is famously known for his "Gaia hypothesis" and Gaia principles. This "green" man of science, born in 1919 and a longtime supporter of nuclear energy, is not formally employed by any government, corporation, or organization.

Sporting one of the most distinguished lists in academia, this U.K. native, upon completion for his work in the U.S., established himself as an "independent" in 1964. During an interview of this past decade, he was 93 and in perfect health, having still all of his wits keenly about him. Lovelock has worked with large corporations, as well as with NASA and high level security agencies. Among his many impressive associations he was a pioneering member of scientists who analyzed CFC's (chlorofluorocarbons), found to be causing a hole in the ozone layer.

James Lovelock's notoriety (which can be found on YouTube) swings from brilliance to blunder and though this is par for the course among physicists his career continues in popular controversy. His insistence that Chernobyl caused only 45 deaths makes this evident, when in contrast it has now been found that the surrounding regions suffered some 500,000 deaths out of as many as 2 million being affected.

He began working for Shell in 1963 having regular meetings with the then Shell boss Lord Rothschild. Lovelock also did a hitch at NASA's Jet Propulsion Lab in Houston, while meeting often with CIA officers in Washington to discuss "electron capture" technology. He was later associated with DARPA, a U.S. Defense Department organization. On his return to London he was invited to present his ideas at a meeting in Century House, but Lovelock failed to mention that it was then also the home to MI6. Later he was invited to Leconsfield House where again, Lovelock glosses over the fact that this Curzon Street address was also the home to MI5.

In his most controversial news interview Lovelock makes a mighty big splash. Whether he is in agreement with, for lack of better words, the "survival belt" prediction which has quietly been gaining traction, I could not find evidence to. The prediction's estimate believes that by the start of the next century only the regions between the 50th and 60th degrees longitude parallels north shall offer any remaining conditions for human habitation. This is an area I have coined as "Eden's belt", or "The Belt of Eden".

Lovelock's interview makes clear that living the way that we do now, the Earth can only support 1 billion people, maybe less. He insinuates that climate change signals an irreversible process which, along with wars, disease, possible pandemics and civil unrest, will cause more than 5 billion people to die by the year 2100, or 84 years from this writing. During the interview he insists it will take a miracle to stop it from happening.

He quickly attacks the renewable energy industry as being a complete waste of time and money and explains we should be preparing the people for this destined outcome instead. Things like taking in more immigrants to the U.K., which Lovelock hints, still has room at the inn. He also compares the survivable regions to being much like a lifeboat; once it's full we must say "no", or all onboard will perish.

I won't make a "conspiracy theory" here, but rather an "educated guess". You see Lovelock did something very peculiar after announcing this far reaching proclamation. He abruptly out of the blue, completely reversed his prediction, downplaying it all as another great miscalculation. This was of course followed by another new book of his to profit from. I'm guessing that MI6 paid Mr. Lovelock a visit and a brief conversation might have went like this, "So Sir James, it seems you've got Her Majesty's royal family throwing a fit, what with all this talk about a 'dooms day', increasing immigration to the Kingdom and what not. Here, here, you're not dabbling with that ghastly LSD stuff again are you? So I tell you what old man, you can immediately reverse your hypothesis publicly and we'll let you live to see another day, or you can watch your family die an extremely painful death one by one, before we get to you. Say, I just thought of something; you know old man if you were a good sort about it all, I'm betting you could even line your pockets a bit writing another book about it! So dear chap, tell us it will be so, or your dear sweet wife and siblings shall all be toast and marmalade by morning".

Areas in the northeastern U.S. have reported Spring is now arriving weeks later than just 150 years ago. Aside from the roar heard above global conferences and government reports the change in climate seems directly related to all of consuming creatures. And the shear extravagance the West alone has afforded itself is quite vulgar and disgraceful to observe. A case in point, one person in Bangladesh uses 300 watts of power a year. His American counterpart uses 12,000. From Smart Buildings to Green Buildings, to Sustainability Management, the battle cry to at least, greatly postpone our doom is now charging ahead at ever greater speeds.

The amount of electricity in the U.S. which today comes from renewable resources, is 13%. The costs of ratcheting that percentage up to 100% is estimated to cost $15 trillion, or about $45,000 for every American. This is the equivalent to more than 150,000 offshore wind turbines, for land based wind farms, 325,000 (each with blades longer than 100 yards), 45,000 solar plants and 75,000 solar rooftop systems.

Along with the change in climate comes change in water, both saltwater and fresh. Oceans which cover 70% of our planet, soak up most of the human-generated CO_2 and energy from the sun. This affects temperature changes, while jeopardizing various organisms and marine life. Ocean levels may rise as much as 20" in just the next 30 years. Urban growth is forecast to increase at least 50% during the next 35 years. Bolivia's Chacaltaya Glacier completely vanished just 5 years ago, putting pressure on urban areas to provide more water. Increases in carbon dioxide will accelerate its effects on crop migrations, pestilence, fires, flooding, erosion, desert expansions, famine and pests.

And like those U.S. bombs over Syria, which were dropped on nothing, so too the taxpaying consumer will have to develop a discerning eye and educated awareness in protecting one's self from the "green charges" which lay ahead. And if you've walked away from "climate change" thinking it's all going to be warm-and-fuzzy, as in a National Geographic's magazine version, just remind yourself that it's now owned by Rupert Murdoch's NewsCorp.

Through it all and with the grace of your God, humankind just might pull a hat trick over this whole fate of ours. One must continue to have hope and above all, bring the "life-surviving issues to the forefront NOW"! Like "stop the damn wars this minute and put that money towards civilization's survival, not destruction"! And "it's high time that we all face population control head on; this means all religions too"!

Working together, yet separately we can develop our own mental capacities, history, identities, cultural uniqueness and solutions, forming civilizations with a much clearer perception and a contented, harmonic balance of the multipolar worlds, both taking shape and yet to come.

Chapter 2

Empires, Corporations, Planet Change and Innovation

In the realm of institutions, commercial corporations are fairly new to the scene. Their existence spans only some 500-700 years, a mere spec of time for the civilization of humankind. During their lifespan as generators of material wealth, they have enjoyed some impressive achievements. In the near future, as the developing nations of the multipolar worlds aspire to raise their standards of living, these institutions will be a key player to the process.

Seeing corporations in their real and exposed potential, most have proven to be utter failures, or lame horses falling short. Too often they remain in their primitive stage, utilizing only a small percentage of their capabilities. As statistics show, the average lifespan of a multinational lasts only some 40 to 50 years. One third of those listed in the 1970 fortune 500 had disappeared by 1983, through mergers, acquisitions, or break-ups. There are few corporations who manage to out-live an average human being.

However, there are at least two that deserve honorable mention, such as the Stora Company. Some 700 years ago it got its start in Sweden as a copper mine, before becoming a prominent chemical, pulp and paper producer. Another century trotter is the Suitomo Group, founded by Riemon Soga in 1590. It originated as a copper casting shop. But we must not forget, that regardless of their soundness and size, the span of 40 years appears to accurately reflect large corporations' average life.

The highest failure rate comes during the first 10 years. In many countries, 40% of them fail during this period. A study by the Stratix Group of Amsterdam, of all companies in Japan and Europe of any size, showed that 12.5 years was the average duration. We can safely assume that they fared no better in the United States. This great disparity, 12.5-to-40-to-700 is both astonishing and bleak. It wreaks hardship and upheaval in working class families, economies and communities. The U.S. alone is riddled with boom-bust, one horse ghost towns.

Royal Dutch Shell (RDS), one of the top three largest corporations globally and based in both the U.K. and the Netherlands, consists of more than 300 companies which are represented in at least 100 countries worldwide. In 1983 they conducted a study and while doing so, it was discovered that companies fail largely due to their management's tunnel vision, infatuation with the economics of goods and services production. It has been commented that the establishments of business education, law and finance were also guilty of this futile practice.

The RDS study then began to fine-tune their criteria which best fit "largest and longest living", of which they found 40 corporations. Of these, 27 were studied in detail and at the end of their study they found four major characteristics:

1: Long-lived companies were sensitive to their environment. They at all times, remained closely in tune to whatever was going on around them. Regardless of the geopolitical, economic, societal, or military turbulence that was echoing in the wind. They always managed to keep a close and very aware, harmonic balance with their environment.

2: Long-lived companies were cohesive, with a strong sense of identity. Regardless of to what degree their diversity expanded, its staff and even its supply people, were made to feel they were all an inclusive part of the whole. It was realized that a strong connection to its people was a vital element, during the navigation of changing times. This cohesiveness also favored a practice of promoting from within. It reflected a sense of longevity in and of itself, as well as membership. A manager's chief concern in such an environment, was always the health of the organization, in its complete body.

3: Long-lived companies were tolerant. They rejected any centralized control over diversification and often permitted marginal occurrences. They kept a wise understanding for different-drummers, eccentricity and experiments just inside the boundaries. It was this wisdom in toleration which later expanded the understanding of fresh possibilities.

4: Long-lived companies were conservative in financing. They were quite spendthrift and didn't dispense their funds foolishly. A natural, yet old-fashioned respect for their funds, were always maintained. These companies were quick to realize the advantages in having reserves and they valued the advantages in their ability to use in-house funds in remaining competitive. This also freed them from the limited terms and leveraged vulnerability of using financiers. Their agility, thanks to saving well, also proved to award them an added advantage in staying abreast of the competition. They could seize more opportunities without having to appease bankers.

Equally valuable lessons can also be learned in observing the many things "they didn't do". Little attention was paid to quarterly profits, or the percentages earned for shareholders. In fact, the study revealed this played no role in the lifespan of the longest living corporations. The prosperity of a company was recognized as a vital sign to its health, but never as a prediction or determination. One should also realize that even though these companies are still in existence today, they lived over half their duration with hand written spread sheets. Like money, they realized the value of their various financial statements, but they also practiced the wisdom that these were records "of the past tense".

In other words, they never lost the capability to connect with the present tense; the ability and reverence to "be here now". As stated in the Royal Dutch Shell study, the spread sheets of GM, Philips Electronics and IBM, during the 70's, did not render them one clue to the trouble which laid ahead of them, 10 years later. Once the trouble rears its ugly head on the financial statement, it's already too late to take preventative action.

A company's country, product, industry, or assets were also found to be irrelevant to its lifespan. It becomes evident that a major gist to the longevity of corporations, is possessing and maintaining a conditioned ability to survive over long segments of time, turbulent with change, while always remaining capable to demonstrate the skillful talents to manage change. Remaining attuned to one's company surroundings, while possessing a conditioned agility to adapt. Creating an impressionable sense of belonging and a value to each other, no matter how small.

Keeping a firm brake on any attempts to centralize diversification, while permitting an open-mindedness to the perceptions of those members who think near the boundary lines. All this, while gently honing the ability to sense moments when it is time to save and when it is time to spend.

Considering the list of indicators of an empire's cultural and moral decline, would it be a safe assumption to disagree that the United States has entered the phase of decadence? The strong currents of social and cultural decay set forth in the 60's of America, has subsided somewhat recently. As you can read in my third book "BRICS and Mortar" it is not anyone's fault, fore it has since been proven that it was the CIA who launched the "drug culture" upon American society with a total sum of $25 million dollars. You see those elite extremists were beginning to implement their destabilization project, not long after Kennedy was out of their way.

The percentage of divorce, abortion, drug abuse, illegitimate births, violent crime and welfare dependency, have fallen and risen at a more delayed pace. Some of these statistics of decline serve as a barometer of good results and not just with a negative read-out. For example, when educated immigrants arrive with skills, immigration can become beneficial to America economically, while it opens up more opportunities from their origin countries, from where they came.

It is in these current times while major, historic shifts in international geopolitics and economy are in play that makes these signs much more difficult to read. Immigrants coming late in the game are only now realizing some of the astonishing irony in these major shifts. Most of them have been breast fed that all of America is like it was in 1963. The famous guitar legend and film producer Ry Cooder, once wrote a very beautiful song that sums this up quite poetically. From some of the lines to his song "Across the Borderline", it goes:

> There's a place where I've been told
> every street is paved with gold
> and it's just across the borderline

And when it's time to take your turn
here's a lesson you should learn
you can lose more, than you ever hope to find

And when you've reached the broken-Promised Land
every dream slips through your hands
then you'll know, it's too late to change your mind

Fore you've slaved so hard to come so far
just to find out where you are
and you've come, just across the borderline.

In failing to decipher between the brainwashing of their parents and the changes in global wealth distribution, there stood some 30,000 Chinese garment workers in San Francisco. After experiencing a much improved and better quality of life for a bit less than a decade, 25,000 of them eventually became unemployed. Their jobs it seemed, were undercut by the very land from whence they came. Shortly afterwards, they quickly began to learn, just what America was really all about.

The current flow of immigrants into the U.S., legal or otherwise, is comparable to the influx which arrived during the early 1900's, only with a reverse effect. Presently they are more inclined to be a dividing force rather than a melting pot.

Let's remind ourselves of the 6 steps of an empire's decline by Sir John Bagot Glubb (Glubb Pasha) in the previous chapter. His sequential order was:

1: pioneering age

2: an age of conquest

3: the age of commerce

4: followed by affluence

5: intellect

6: decadence and decline

 Remember, the key element to the new worlders' methods; "division". You might begin to notice a "unipolar creep" since the first things which come to mind are "destabilization" and "disuniting". The gross dissimilarity between the immigrants of the 1900's to present day is the overall adaptation of "multiculturalism" by the "intellectual" American elite. The promoting of immigrants to transplant their culture, rather than assimilate into the national existing one, is fragmentation and not the melding of a variety fused into one unity. History has proven that the union of cultures unequivocally ends like a collision of opposing charges, clashing in opposition.

 It may be foolhardy to assume that America will magically side-step with Teflon slippers, the experiences suffered by the fallen empires of the past. Intelligent as we are, things seem easy enough to fix. "If" we are permitted to. I would beg to differ that this moment in time is a revelation. I'm more inclined to agree that this period has all the characteristics of being orchestrated and implanted. To remain exempt from "conspiracy theorizing", I would call it a contingency. To be force-fed decadence while being deprived of the future's opportunity is totalitarian ideology and not a consensus. The adamant self-denial of neocon extremists, now woven into the foundational fabric of the new America, exhibits an abnormal disparity, in contrast to the global geopolitical majority of today.

 Immense prosperity could be gained and shared by all in the West and the time to seize that moment certainly is now. Its requirements crave for somethings never tried before. Picture if you will, if Rome or Greece had drastically accelerated a reduction to the size of their empires and the scope of their control, "ahead of their decline". America's situation demands an admission and acceptance to be made domestically whole again; not as a global conquistador.

To become much smaller, more agile and a leaner universal team player. It is in dire need of losing weight and demonstrating wisdom and discretion and to stop bullying. Its last chance has arrived to start striking constructive partnerships with old enemies and abandon the practices of destruction and destabilization, repent its mistakes, repair them with its own people's ingenuity and innovative talents, chart a new "positive" course and be done with this thing they call domination.

Fate has been whispering into the ears of America until it is hoarse, that it's time to acknowledge this is the moment to "pass the baton" to a younger runner and whose time has come undeniably. It's not time for America to be great again, it's time for America to "get small"! Time to let others police the world; better yet, allow them to police themselves. The 50 year stretch of esoteric doctrines is what's pulling America towards its demise. The resonance of economic, gravitational forces are delivering a clear message. In unison with the 9 planets, earthlings' chances for long-term survival, rests clearly on the orbiting of multipolar systems, all sharing in tandem the same orbital paths, each at their own degrees of incline, time and space.

Should the failed policies of a unipolar world persist, the West will cause a cosmic crack-of-the-whip. This reaction will force its trade winds and geopolitical existence to shift at a greater and greater momentum, to a distance away from all nations. There it will find itself alone and abandoned as a barren moon.

There's a variety of economics which few have yet to explore. It's "astrological economics". Economists have stated that in 2007 we entered a global recession, which was just before Pluto entered Capricorn. They interpret that the U.S. recession began to end in 2009, but they contend it took several years before any bonafide signs of growth gained any traction. Capricorn was entered by Pluto creating a contraction which ended the expansion of Pluto moving through Sagittarius. Once Uranus became visible to Pluto in 2011, astrologs believe the global recovery then came into full swing. The relay enabled a process to perceive in a new perception (Uranus) in reconstruction and transformation (Pluto). Once the square between Uranus and Pluto started in 2012, the economic recovery was on the up and up.

According to the Sibley chart, ordinarily used for the U.S., Americans began to become overly optimistic and subsequently fell prey to the absolute faith, or a ballooning effect, during the run-up to the economy of 2008. It is currently true that overall, civilization in America is in the moment of decline. However, from the economic astrolog's perspective, there are no foreseen signals that the 2015-2019 time span will be any more treacherous than anything in recent times.

Uranus and Pluto transported the U.S. mid heaven during 2008-2010. During 2010-2011 the U.S. experienced a "Saturn Return". The econo-astrologs admit there shows great challenges to the U.S. for 2015-2016, in terms of major "identity issues" overall. Nonetheless, they see no particular effects taking place for this period, as it relates to the economy. The time frame these folks seem the most concerned about is the 2020-2023 period. The U.S. fits the 250 year requirement for Pluto's return to its place in the national chart. The requirements of this Pluto cycle demand things of a nation akin to change, transformation, new policies and new government. Pluto will then be in the second house of money for the U.S. chart. In layman's terms, an absolute certainty that the financial system will undergo a major transformation. This will likely begin during 2018 (which ironically coincides with the IMF's intent to initiate a new dollarization plan), while in the meantime the U.S. will be suspended in reality-based economics. (The rigging of markets is real in the U.S., but not "realty-based"). Our astrological economics friends warn that it's a good time to avoid investing in fads, passing circles, or using chain letters. Instead they prescribe that its back to old-fashioned values of prudent spending, hard work and savings, characteristic of Pluto in Capricorn.

In the polarity of international relations, the four popular systems in which power is distributed through the international apparatus are: unipolarity, bipolarity, tripolarity and multipolarity. There also trails a fifth one, "nonpolarity". Unipolarity was a system developed during the post-Cold War as an international operation used by the U.S. with the then Soviet Union as its foe. Though it is both frustrating and absurd, it is important to realize several strategic blunders of the 2015-2016 period. The Soviet Union is no more, just as Mao Zedong's "old China" (this in the economic sense, not the principled sense and is in no way disrespectful of the infamous leader) is past. Both the "new Russian Federation" and the "new China" are some of the most promising, global economic engines of our time, who've fully embraced most capitalist practices. The fall of the Soviet Union witnessed the final days of its Zionist henchmen (it is noteworthy, that it would appear those Zionist henchmen have only relocated to the U.S., in some shape or form).

Gross miscalculations, most made by the U.S. are now interrupting and damaging a natural, global evolution in polarities, growth, intelligence, progress, as well as fiscal health and well-being. The same school of "hate" mongering once associated with the Soviet Union echelon were evicted and/or fled. Their school of thought however has succeeded in massively infecting "the new U.S. Industrial Military Complex". Their reach now permeates throughout America's four major news organizations and its foreign policy-making. This is a great body-block to the progression of prosperity which only benefits a very few, while destroying the host as a whole. It also classifies for there no longer being any "actual news", only a monotonous, repetitive, prescribed compounding of propaganda. America's Network news Zionist owners have insisted on using an old Nazi practice, whereby "if you repeat the same lies long enough, people will start to believe them".

So the natural, cosmic, geopolitical evolution of the "new U.S.", which both desires and needs the cooperative elements of the multipolar system, has been terrorized and forced backward in time, to the pre-Cold War period. In "reality" this is not possible and it is only the dreams of madmen such as Zbigniew Brzezinski, William Kristol, Dick Cheney and Robert Kagan. Hence, its persistence to cling to a unipolar system continues. Unipolarity is anarchical. Nuno P. Monteiro, Assistant Professor of Political Science at Yale University, states that this anarchy, "..., results from the incomplete power preponderance of the unipole". Monteiro cites Columbia University's Kenneth Waltz who argues, "A great power cannot exert a positive control everywhere in the world". So in our present modern era, unipolarity is made antiquated. Its system adapted from olden times, where only one great power faced no competition.

American's ineptitude to give push-back and regain control of their government to steer their future, now leads them to a precarious fork in the road; both are dangerous. Currently, America's people choosing to "doing nothing" is what makes the two remaining options both evil. Now, either their Zionist handlers will take their never-ending lust for war against the people themselves, as in the totalitarian era leading up to the Bolshevik Revolution and the "new U.S." is forced to be reborn a Fascist State, or the whole charade ends in a nuclear war, where nobody wins.

On October 3, 2001 Israeli Prime Minister Ariel Sharon stated, "We the Jewish people control America and the Americans know it". In December of 2008 Jewish columnist Joel Stern wrote in the Los Angeles Times, "I don't care if Americans think we're running the news media, Hollywood, Wall Street, or the government. I just care that we get to keep running them".

If, like the Bolsheviks, Americans have lost their country to organized Zionist Jewry, they lost it quietly and unaware. Most of sheepish America still remains unaware that their country no longer belongs to them. Solzhenitsyn, in "The Gulag Archipelago" cites that 66 million Russian Christians were tortured and put to death. Those who devised the torture and the orders to rape and kill ethnic Russians were predominantly Jews. Out of the 388 members of the new revolutionary government in Russia, only sixteen were actually Russian. Aside from one black, 371 were Jews. These revolutionaries hid their Jewish identities by changing their names. From Ulyanov to Lenin, Bronstein to Trotsky, Apfelbaum to Zinoviev, Solomon to Sverdlov, Wallach to Litvonov, Rosenfeld to Kamenev, Helphand to Parvus, Zederbaum to Martov, Nathanson to Bohrin and the list goes on. Under Stalin, if one even drew attention to the fact that unpopular officials were Jewish, it meant the death penalty. All was largely funded by America's Zionist Wall Street banker Jacob Schiff. Germany, Russia, they both had their hour in the sun and fell under Jewish hegemony. It's now America's turn. Israeli Prime Minister Benjamin Netanyahu, in 2002 stated, "Once we squeeze all we can out of the United States, it can dry up and blow away".

Some glaring evidence to the flaws of the unipolar system are found in the first two decades of the post-Cold War existence. Having been defined as unipolar, it was riddled with wars. For 13 of the 22 years since the end of the Cold War, the United States has been at war. In other words, though the first twenty years of unipolarity make up less than 10% of U.S. history, they account for more than 25% of the nation's complete time at war. Multipolarity constitutes more than two nation States having nearly equal amounts of military, cultural and economic influence in a distribution of power.

Classical realist theorists like Hans Morgenthau and E.H. Carr attest that multipolar systems are more stable, enabling the replenishment of powers through alliances. The Cold War's end muffled the 1980's popular debate over America's possible decline and in turn triggered a new debate concerning unipolarity. In the aftermath of the Great Recession a verdict can now be reached on those debates. As it turns out, the declinists had it right all along. For one obvious example, the U.S. share of global GDP shrunk to a mere 18% by 2014, well below post-World War II figures of 22%-25%. As the declinists had predicted, chronic budget and account deficits, over consumption, under savings and deindustrialization have all exasperated their toll on America's economy. It's time for the West to bury its hatchets and cease behaving as an inebriated Neanderthal, mad on grog.

Judgement can now be concluded on the debate, between the balance of power realists and the unipolar stability theorists. As balance of power realists had claimed, one great new power has already emerged to act as a counterbalance to America, with others waiting in the wings. Unipolarity stability theorists erred because they used "static measures" of national power, failing to grasp the rapidity of China's rise. China's GDP passing the U.S. in 2016 being a direct example. No longer is China emerging, it has "risen". The debate over unipolarity is a closed case.

The power distribution of the international system shifts dramatically now. U.S. strategy must now respond to the new multipolar constellation constructively, being beneficial to partnering without antiquated posturing, seeing eye to eye, never to look downward. Yet security study students and U.S. policymakers are in a panic to a neurotic form of denialism. Firstly, they cannot bring themselves to accept it. Secondly, even when proven that unipolarity has ended they adopt a myopic dream that "Pax Americana" will prevail, even though it's buttressed by nothing.

Profound consequences always follows hegemonic decline. The American citizenry stands to be greatly fleeced and imprisoned away from an enormous prosperity if theorists are correct and it takes ten to fifteen years to manage this change. Some of that citizenry has already seen the writing on the wall. They are choosing to leapfrog their policymakers, even if it means taking a job in a multipolar country.

Trending as we speak, people from various nations around the world have cotton-balled their ears to the Western drums of "hate" campaigns and are becoming Russian citizens. Western Zionist press seems to ever trumpet about bears in the streets of Russian cities and Putin regime boogiemen, blah, blah, blah. Some of this enlightened and low-key migration sports some famous faces. French actor Gerard Depardieu, American athlete Roy Jones, Fred Durst is talking about it, Olympic boxing champion Lennox Lewis, to name a few. Foreign journalists and T.V. personnel are also hitching a ride, as well as snowboarder Vie Wild, short track champion Viktor Ahn, Japanese skater Yuko Kawaguti and two American basketball players Rebecca Hammon and Deanna Nolan. The list includes athletes, journalists, actors, balloonists, scientists and inventors.

And just what reasoning propels such a wide swath of Western talent to jump ship? The answers reveal that the West has taken the principles of tolerance and political correctness to disproportionate, grotesque forms, making it difficult for people to live. In the search for freedom, Europe and America have come to a point which is referred to as "liberal totalitarianism" and a dictation of minorities. The people see it and do not wish to live in it – they pack their bags bound for Russia – a country of traditional values in a sea of ultra-liberalism. Apparently the identity of Russia being cold and wild has become vague. People are realizing today's Russia has become a lot more comfortable for them to live and work.

Once defectors used to come to the U.S. in search for the American Dream. Many are now sadly confessing that it's been reduced to just that, "a dream". The foreign migration to Russia for "the Russian Dream" is said to offer more substance. Its new citizens I'm told, will become real patriots as it's not difficult to love Russia. Loving Russia seems easy, pleasant and natural. Something else I should mention. Simply put, "it loves you back".

While the process of multipolar separation gives rise to various orbiting degrees of geopolitical and economic, global distribution, researchers are smashing proton beams near the speed of light. Situated between 150-500 feet underground in France, near the border to Switzerland, the Large Hadron Collider (LHC) is 17 miles in circumference and can thrust protons to make revolutions through its gigantic tube at some 11,000 times-per-second. As the LHC affords physicists the study of Big Bang, the "Higgs bosun" and the missing pieces to the theories which govern particle physics, there's a long wish list within this ever-expanding phenomena of knowledge. The possibilities could send goose bumps up the spines of any George Noory, David Icke, or James Locklock groupie. So finite is the monitoring of this behemoth that it is fitted with a 66 million channel Pixer Tracker in its Compact Muon Solenoid.

The LHC could definitely expose the way to new scientific frontiers, such as additional dimensions in space, new basic forces of nature, or the hidden supersymmetric particles. Fermilab physicist Don Lincoln states, "Our best possible scenario is that we see supersymmetric, we see extra dimensions, we see evidence of dark matter" (which 96% of the universe is made up of). Science fans are even speculating about the possibilities for LHC to open a portal to a parallel universe, but Lincoln says such claims are misleading.

At a construction cost of $10 billion, its research center known as CERN reports that particle beams were successfully flung around the LHC in two directions, after a two year shutdown. Studies of the many billions of collisions during LHC's first run (2010-2013) gave evidence of the "Higgs bosun" and its connecting force field, a long sought after mechanism that gives matter its mass. CERN reports the 2 year LHC shutdown was for a major refit, a Herculean task, which has now equipped the LHC with the doubling of its power and its peer into the unknown. Scientists are now anticipating the discovery in signs of the "New Physics".

Beneath the French village of St. Genis Pouilly, near Geneva, the concepts of "dark matter" and SUSY (supersymmetry) receives constant and careful pondering. Oliver Buchmueller is a scientist stationed at one of the four collision monitoring machines around the LHC. He commented, "If I had to bet on what we'll find, I would go for SUSY. But we could find something very, very unexpected".

The CERN – LHC collaboration, which includes over 10,000 scientists and engineers from more than 100 countries, in conjunction with hundreds of universities and laboratories, should prove some remarkable and historic results. The LHC's computing grid is a world's record, which connects 140 computing centers in 35 countries, consisting of 170 computing facilities, through a worldwide network across 36 nations. Among other studies that will utilize CERN's LHC are the composition and aspects of "quark-gluon plasma", which is believed to have existed in the early universe.

The geoengineering fixers of climate are upon us. While the plans were still in the designing stages for CERN's LHC, clear across the globe and much deeper underground, a prenominal event was brewing. During the late afternoon of April 2, 1991, on Luzon Island in the Philippines, Mt. Pinatubo started rumbling with a number of steam explosions. Having been dormant for over 400 years, Mt. Pinatubo was not even on most volcanic scientist's radar screen. Steam explosions are characteristics leading up to eventual eruption and for two months they released intermittent warnings. On June 15, 1991 the mountain exploded with an intensity of thrust which sent molten lava flinging at speeds of six hundred miles per hour. Two hundred thousand people were forced to evacuate, with flooding lava spreading 250 square miles.

Hours later a plume of ash and gas pierced the stratosphere, extending twenty-one miles high. In the weeks that followed, a cloud of aerosol surrounded the planet where it lingered for over a year. More than 18 million metric tons of sulfur dioxide blended with water, creating a mirror of gas causing the Sun's rays to return into the heavens. For the entire months of 1992-1993 there was a 10% reduction for the amount of sunlight reaching Earth's surface. Human industrial activities have, over the past century, caused a rise in the planet's temperatures. However slight, they set into motion a chain reaction of events which can last for years.

For example, this one volcano alone can effect rain patterns, drought, floods, wildfires and crop productions for several years. Some are beginning to argue that humankind has shift Earth into a long, irreversible process of self-correction. Like a pinball sent in endless motion, which never gutters. A continuous mounting set of chain reactions in perpetual collision. Scientist's largest fear is in the feasibility of Artic permafrost's melting. If this should occur, it would release vast, lethal amounts of methane gas into the atmosphere. If such a possibility becomes reality, hydrologists say "its game over".

Shifting away from the bleakest scenario, to a more bearable tint with an economic hue, the verdict on how climate change will affect the global economy is in. According to a Tuft's University study, should climate change continue to follow its current models of behavior, planet-wide economic production would tumble some 23% by the year 2100. The ramifications of the planet's adjustments in adapting to human habitation and how it correlates to a nation's economy, will prove to be a very challenging and transitional shift. My own personal deduction is that this mentioned verdict is dead wrong and "off the mark". I will wager that any projected losses from traditional production, will easily be made up in "new industries" which have not been added into the Tuft's equation. I also think that it is a shameful demonstration of how present day, Western academia is selling its students short by insisting to keep them locked up in antiquated, unipolar, mind-conditioning programs, geared only for short-sighted corporations whom its students will well outlive.

The climatic effects however, will be inescapable for most. It will require extremely elevated adaptation skills for both individuals and businesses. Many key leaders in industries will find themselves having to lead their targets well, while taking aim at any future objectives, in an ever-shifting and migrating environment. Yes it will be rough-and-tumble and yes it will mean being situated any-which-way-but-loose, but ah I can guarantee you it will be anything, but boring!

Once lush environments will slowly transform into new desert lands, while once unfarmed places will become tomorrow's bread baskets. Workforce shifts will give cause to an exodus, as they surrender to the toiling with fires, floods and storms and migrate to more fertile, sounder environments which still offer a more balanced sense of stability. The irony in "planet change" as a global prognosis is, it will prove to be the first time in human history innovation needn't use the excuse of war to force it to the forefront. It is because planet change in and of itself, automatically makes every person of every nation at war in combating our own effects upon the earth for our very survival. "Ethical investing" too, will finally have its day in the sun.

With a greater need for innovation comes the need for better companies. To get familiarized with what some of those companies might look like, the following are some examples of companies today who have a growing reputation for innovation. This is purely from an operational standpoint and they have not been litmus-tested for any green appeal. Baidu, China's most successful search engine, was founded by Robin Li in 2000. It has a market cap of $71.4 billion with a 46,391 employees and sales of $7.95 billion. For the first quarter its mobility accounted for 50% of total revenues, while its online payment services "Baidu Wallet" has 26 million active users. Its food service delivery was launched a year ago and is the market leader in more than 35 cities, with an active presence in 70 cities. While companies like Microsoft and Tesla grow fearful and apprehensive of artificial intelligence, Baidu's Andrew Ng, who formerly led the "Google Brain" deep learning project, is now spearheading Baidu's $300 million AI Lab.

Ng raises the question "what if". What if for instance, while we taught machines to think we also taught them somethings about cooperation and how to get along not only with us, but with other machines? Baidu has a characteristic of pressing hypothetical situations on its employees. The culture often makes attempts at bridging the theoretical to the actual. The multiple choices of this equation, which Baidu's management has a reputation for, has instilled a forward thinking in both its leadership and in a trickledown effect onto all its employees. It coaxes workers into a problem-solving way of thinking, whereby the final solutions can be taught to robots.

The current explosion and encouragement of innovation underway in China, sets it a distant breed apart from its Asian neighbor Japan. The elementary foundations to Japan's economic moment in the Sun offered scarce examples of its own contributions. Most of its manufacturing formats were taken from the American models of Edward Deming, an American who corporate America laughed out of town, only to become "The Father of Japanese Manufacturing". To this day, corporate America has still been kicking itself for not truly listening to Deming and is still preaching his old models, even though they are now 25 years behind current times. The extent of Japan's engineering feats were not much beyond glorified versions of reverse-engineering enhancements.

Brazil being one of the chief darlings of the BRICS nations, seems well positioned in being a leading innovator for an increasingly connected and collaborative multipolar world. Brazilians avidly adopt digital technologies which leveraged the creative potential of the herd. Their styles of utilization are steering an accelerated, more efficient innovation. Having the world's third largest amount of Facebook users, many of its small businesses and startups continue to reshape Latin America's innovative landscape. It should be noted here, that it is discussed in-depth in my third book, "BRICS and Mortar" the many profound reasons why one should now "abandon Facebook", as it is currently being used as a "mind-control" apparatus for U.S. affiliates with U.S. government intelligence agencies.

With "collaboration" being the molten hot buzz word on innovative companies' front burners today, Brazilians have an interesting "trust deficit". In 2014 the country's National Confederation of Industry took a survey. In it they discovered that 62% of Brazilians responded they had little or no trust in most people. In a deeper analysis of a 4 year Interpersonal Trust Index study, Brazil placed 54th of 59 participating nations, in terms of the degree in which people trusted others around them.

In an Accenture survey of top executives they were posed the question of how they would approach expanding their businesses into other areas. Seventy-two percent of them responded, through "in-house" ventures. On the Global Innovation Index, compiled by Cornell, INSEAD Business School and The World Intellectual Property Organization, Brazil placed 61st out of 143 countries.

Yet these statistics give pause for thought. When you have a failing, fading, debt-ridden unipolar world Brazil is wise to be cautious. Polarities are shifting and that means there's never been a better time for one to hold their cards close to their chest. Many statistical campaigns of the West are more inclined to resemble "intimidating propaganda", which once translated means "we've run plum out of ideas of our own, so we thought we'd steal some of yours". Not to sound overly paranoid here, but the reality in Latin America has always been a hotbed for Western, Cold War espionage. The West's CIA has a notorious reputation in Latin America, along with its cousins the World Bank and the IMF, who are constantly trying to undermine Latin America's success, in the name of its dinosaur, New World Order supporters. It comes as no small wonder then, that the majority of the world's "bank robbers' have all been American (with the Rothschilds perhaps being an exception to the rule).

When ambassadors and pundits from the unipolar universe of slime, begin using words like they're "concerned" or "worried" about your ability to open up, it more than likely means that you're doing just fine and that's actually what's got them worried. I personally am no fan of Accenture who demonstrates the behavior of a global-maniac, with little to no considerations for local cultures and too often possesses a highly disposable sense of perception.

Nonetheless, Embraco comes to mind when thinking about Brazilian innovation. Being the world's largest makers of compressors, it partnered with the New Zealand company Fisher and Paykel, an appliance maker to develop the world's first refrigerator compressor that works without lubricants. According to Embraco's R&D director the company is now positioned for industry leadership, in a future where refrigerators will have no compressors at all.

RVC is a development institute and fund of funds. It is a strategic tool of the Russian Federation for building its own national Innovation system. Being established in 2006, its purpose is to promote creation of Russian venture financial resources for venture capital funds. RVC's investment activity involves private Russian and foreign participants in the innovation sections of Russia's economy, while developing new investment tools of the national venture capital market. This activity is made possible, by establishing funds based on private and public partnership. Focus on knowledge-intensive, high-risk industrial sectors, RVC also pays close attention to seed and pre-seed funds.

Its priority areas are security, living systems, nanosystems' industries, information, sustainable environmental management, transport & power and energy efficiency. As of 2014 RVC assisted fifty Russian companies in entering foreign markets. Unlike its Brazilian BRICS brother, RVC actively seeks development of partnerships with the key players in the most promising international, innovative markets. During 2014 alone some 6,714 innovative projects took part in competitions which were organized and supported by RVC. Its programs' support and development tools cover 39 objects of the innovation infrastructure. RVC consulting services have been provided to some 734 technology companies. Companies like Promobot, Kera-Tech, NanoServ and VeeRoute are just a few examples of promising, innovative corporations, who began their start as contestants in RVC competition sponsorships.

Irony seems to enter into the equation quite often in this book. This time it can be found in "Russian sanctions", something adapted from the school of "Idiot Economics" and the "Foreign Policy Implosion". Sanctions thus far, have proven to have had a "back-firing" effect. They've alienated the U.S. further, while hurting its European allies deeper, all while making Russia doubly better and twice as strong.

Another example in Russian innovation is Rusnano. Its goal for this this year is to create a nano-industry capable of producing $29 billion of marketable products. Though this company is run much like a promising Silicon Valley start-up, it abstains from the extravagance and 100% of Rusnano shares are owned by the government. Its Director General (CEO) is usually appointed by Russia's presidents. It's a joint-stock company, being both a Private Equity and Venture Capital vehicle. Like China's State-controlled companies, Rusnano has no tolerance for "waste", especially when it involves "public monies". And as irony would have it again, due to market forces affecting its capital, Rusnano plans to attract additional investment by issuing State-guaranteed bonds and making 40% of the company private.

VK 's site (available in the U.S.) has tools for managing community and celebrity pages, while enabling its users to upload, search and stream media content, videos and music. Its ease of navigation and agile format places its user satisfaction a notch above Facebook. Its challenges to future innovation will be in remaining competitive without sacrificing any of its core values, its most prominent one being "caution". VK has all the characteristics of a long-life company. It remains loyal to keeping in tune with its surrounding environment and doesn't annoy the user with arrays of useless gadgetry. Thus far, it seems to be well seasoned in balancing the right times to save with the right times to spend. Though it still is well endowed with an avid audience, any future notoriety in innovation will have to come from spearheading more "being 1st in" discoveries to its future.

India's Tata Consultancy Services (TCS) is a multinational IT consulting and solutions for business company, based in Mumbai, India. It has a presence in 46 countries and is one of India's largest companies. TCS is the world's 10th largest IT services provider. The company is equipped with a mind-boggling 250,000 employees with a cross-cut of 113 different nationalities. Dr. Ritu Anand, a TCS vice president, admits to its challenges in cultural diversity, in non-English speaking countries. "There are issues related to language, culture, laws and regulations. It's tough, but achievable". In Latin America TCS has established itself in Argentina, Brazil, Chile, Mexico and Uruguay, with a mix of nationalities at all levels. Its employees relate well to international celebrations and TCS has culture-specific ones, such as Thanksgiving, Chinese New Year, etc., so as to constantly maintain an organic balance within its global dimension. Among a wide spectrum of programs, too long to list, it keeps a culture and gender awareness deeply enriched.

Foreign Language Initiatives (FLI) is a TCS group focusing on cultural integration and language training. All these spectacular considerations for a company of this magnitude, seems an award-winning corporate achievement. An outsider is quick to notice its glaring contrast to old unipolar styles. India being one of the leading nations in the BRICS group of countries, it is easy to see the welcoming appeal and nurturing practical differences from its Western unipolar counterparts.

The West's disposition of "destabilization", "cultural destruction", "anti-sovereignty", "force-fed ideology" and "my way is the only way", makes it no secret as to why many more nations are preparing their great escape to a multipolar way of life.

Some of the contributing factors to a viable and healthy corporate culture, are found in the ones who are innately perceptive and intelligently responsive. Western corporations prominent handicap are in hiring middle and upper management with no hands-on experience, at least at the lower ends of the industry.

These individuals too often possess a fixed, textbook perception, being prone to societal fads of so-called business gurus and trendy, shallow business celebrities. They can make the company's own corporate culture susceptible to cookie-cutter methodologies.

The lack of ground level experience in an organization's upper and mid-level management can create panic decision-making. It can ignite tendencies of hastily resorting to throwing adhoc solutions at problems, with a try-this-or-that, roulette approach. "Bluffing" and "delegating" are highly infectious to managerial leadership and systemically malignant to the body corporate. These aspects also do not permeate a knowingly innovative environment into the corporate culture, only a perplexing one. Too many Western corporations have become dumb-founded, painted brightly with a thin layer of veneer imagery. When they get too dumb, they go out and buy a company who knows more about what it is doing and hope for the best. Mergers and acquisitions very rarely benefit anyone, past the middlemen at the point of sale. They destroy economic growth and spread their viral deficiencies.

I've identified and analyzed six prominent aspects which are most popular in describing "corporate culture" of the modern times. Most are from high-caliber, very expensive Western universities, yet most of them I believe to be wrong. I have listed the leading academic principles in successful corporate culture and if I disagree with them I have explained why and then replaced them with my own. After an in-depth review of the subject matter, here are my findings:

1: <u>Consciousness</u>: Though the majority of Ivy League business colleges today, would replace this with "vision", I both beg to differ and consider it a failed attribute and an outdated trend. "Vision" as you know, lends strong hints to being apparitional, delusional, fantasy-like and dreamy. Not exactly the makings of a solid foundation. I prefer "consciousness" for as you may recall, when we studied some of the secrets to those rare companies who have existed for centuries, "being aware" of your own environment and to what's happening around you, was one of their outstanding traits.

With consciousness being a leading ingredient into a company's culture and mission statement, people immediately feel accepted "in the present tense". Consciousness also correlates that the organization is aware and is more inclined to greet and adapt to change and is in tune with reality; not being in denial about it, or focusing on mirages.

2: <u>Principles</u>: Again, the most expensive business schools in the United States listed "values" in place of this and I must again stand in objection. "Principles" more or less tell everyone what your organization's characteristics are all about, in a list or outline. They also proclaim ethical standards, but give the employee the freedom to portray them in their own style. "Principles" are the sheet-music and you are the instrument.

"Values" on the other hand, are another tried and failed creation of lost corporations from the unipolar universe. Values set guidelines for behavior, breeding "yes-people" and "ass-kissers", with little or no room to express or articulate the artistry of their own imagination. I would conclude that "Principles" would nurture innovation, whereas "values" likely would inhibit a stifling effect.

3: <u>Cohesion</u>: This third foundational block to corporate culture is a bit of the manifestation of all the other parts as a whole. Popular unipolar beliefs would replace this with "Practices", to which I disagree. "Practices" are enshrined values, translated in short means, "Good dog, now here's your bone." Since "principles" preserves the individual members to keep their identity (i.e.: values = blind obedience), "cohesion" plays the role of "a sense of belonging". Cohesion's strength is "appeal" and if you create an appealing environment where members are each appreciated and respected as a vital part of the organic team, without the regimental controls, they will be more willing to concern themselves with the well-being of the whole organization. A healthy cohesiveness also will propagate an organic sense of pride and admired reputation.

4: <u>Money</u>: That unpleasant subject. Actually this is where Western academia insists "People" should be placed. "Money" as a company's culture component, is in the understanding and appreciation of its value. It means having the ability to think on your feet while cultivating a wisdom that can accurately realize when it's a good time to spend. The value of purchases are realized, as well as an understanding of the best times and methods to save. If a corporate culture can feel a natural sense of trust in its money management, it will know and believe that when the time is right, the organization will always be willing to re-invest in its members.

"People" however, as a component of textbook, unipolar theory for corporate culture, always makes the same mistakes by not stating what it is they're really trying to say. Once one digs down underneath the surface they discover that translated, "people" in actuality under Western models means that they don't give a hill of beans about their people at all. They only want those who will "obey without question" and are willing to endure, without complaint, the most disrespectful wages for a maximum profitable output. All prominent, Western business universities "fully embrace the practices of mind control" and the stripping down of the individual's psyche and never to elevate one's self, as a free individual. "Facebook" is only one of the many weapons in their arsenal.

5: <u>Recharge</u>: Again, Western Ivy League colleges replace this building block with "Narrative", the telling and retelling of a company's and/or founder's life struggle, until you're blue in the face and I say "poppycock"! Nowhere in a 700 year history of a surviving corporation was there ever found any evidence of a place for bedtime stories. "Boring"!

"Recharge" however, is key to a corporate culture's vitality. A variable exercise of this for example might include a "mandatory" 1 hour "paid" lunchtime, consisting of 30 minutes for lunch, 15 minutes for the workout of your choice in the company gym, followed by 15 minutes in one of its meditation rooms. This may be done in groups as well, but with no electronic devices whatsoever and no talking. For my 3 years working in China I was given a "2 ½ hour" lunch with a fold-out bed for my afternoon nap. In other countries lunch may be as long as "3 hours". This 1 hour could also be left to the individual, but some kind of "shared" daily activity, whether it's a 10 minute warmup in the morning, or a 10 minute class in the afternoon would be a healthy practice.

I'm not particularly fond of the term "meditation". So whatever it is you wish to call the practice of awarding yourself the time however brief, to put your mind in the "present tense", is a key trace element to mental stability. I've coined my own adage for this. It goes, "When the wise man crosses the river, he sees the water". Yes, in fact when I was writing this book I would walk across a bridge over a river, maybe several times a week and I always made it a point to look at the river, see its rocks, maybe look for fish, etc. It is a sad thing when the majority of our daily lives are taken hostage by either the preoccupation with the past tense, or anticipation of the future.

6: <u>Tolerance</u>: With this last major foundation block for building the best (and hopefully perpetual) corporate culture, the misleading bastions of unipolar dogmatists (Western universities) would want me to replace this one with "Place". Place is a fishbowl and you can package it in whatever fancy architecture you wish, but at the end of the day as the New York singer-song writer Michael Packer used to say, "it's the same old garbage, in a brand new truck". Innovation, quality, creative thinking and pioneering concepts demand the knowledge and contributions of all members, no matter how different or aloof they might appear to others.

The multipolarity of brilliance is born from the "what if" people, who are oftentimes stretching the boundaries and flirting with the edges. The foolhardiness of unipolarity is sensationalistic. It is prone to fads, hoopla, atmosphere and a "build it and they will come" stigma. Studies have already proven time and again, that whether you wish to locate your business on First Street in San Jose, California, or Wall Street in New York, or on the side of a mountain in Timbuctoo, location and architecture haven't squat to do with building the best corporate culture outside of local logistics.

Some basic elements of unipolarity disposition are obedience, conformity, imbalance and explosion. Its non-conforming members are lined up and fired. This creates an explosive and unhealthy imbalance and a rippling effect. I once worked for 7 years in a very famous fashion apparel organization. The facility consisted of 330 employees. After 7 years I was only one of the 40 surviving, original members. The remaining 290 workers found themselves getting fired or quitting. Also during those 7 years, I went through 9 managers who also all were fired, or quit. One woman I knew was so stressed out that she forgot to turn her head to look out into oncoming traffic, as she left the driveway and was instantly killed in an accident. I was also cross-trained in 11 different departments, not knowing what I'd be doing and for whom every day. It was the most highly disposable environment I've ever encountered, but I came out a survivor.

Multipolarity disposition is an imploding force which levitates all within, in a healthy balance. People go to work at these types of corporations with smiles on their faces with some even showing up earlier than needed. It is this organic culture which attracts talent like a magnet, because its members are naturally appreciated and permitted to be themselves. I would hope these examples should lend ample enough fodder to anyone breaking ground for their foundational blocks to a healthy corporate culture.

Finding itself with one of the fastest growing economies in the multipolar universe, Chile has found itself in the predicament of attempting to support rapid economic growth while refraining from the over exploitation of its natural resources that sparked its launch. Monte Alto Renovable (MAR) strives to provide extensive biomass energy services to businesses and municipalities near Torres del Paine National Park, in the Chilean Patagonia. MAR assists these businesses and townships in managing the initial costs of renewable energy. Their win-win solution is achieved by financing and providing a full spectrum of energy services that includes equipment purchases, installations, fuel supply and maintenance in swaps for long-term energy supply contracts. MAR intends to phase out 1 million kilowatt hours of diesel energy with biomass fuel, enabling it to extinguish emissions of 6,000 – 8,000 tons of Carbon dioxide each year. Every client will experience a savings of $20,000 to $50,000 a year in fuel costs.

Being a revolutionary concept for Latin America, MAR sets a business model example, as an accomplished and pioneering energy services company for the future. Its project will greatly boost two major elements in the local economy, forestry and tourism. Monte Alto Forestal S.A. is a local, integrated forestry company founded in 1929 by the Mladinic Beros brothers, in the lenga forests. In 2008 the American based Global Environmental Fund made a significant contribution to MAF S.A. and actively works with the Mladinic family in providing managerial assistance and strategic planning.

Russia's fourth largest mobile phone operator Yota, not only provides broadband services, but also manufactures its own smartphone. Yota is a trademark of Skartel. It is owned by one of the three national mobile phone operators MegaFon, the other two being MTS and Beeline. The company currently operates in both Moscow and St. Petersburg with plans for nationwide expansion.

Yota's firm aims to acquire 10 million network clients over the next three years, according to Skartel's CEO Anatoly Smorgonsky. Basic subscriber packages with an unlimited number of calls within the network plus 300 minutes of free calls to other networks, will cost $21 in Moscow and about $17 in St. Petersburg.

The Yota brand is oriented toward advanced internet users, so it will not duplicate MegaFon's services. The market segments of this industry are always under tough competition. Today Yota users have access to LTE standard internet services in nine cities of Russia. Yota's 4G is now available in 180 Russian cities.

Thinking of what country you should base your new corporation? If you're still orbiting the Sun from unipolar America, consider this. The IMF has applauded U.K. Conservatives for their resilient efforts following the British Social Party's brush with disaster. The necessary measures implemented by Chancellor Osborne were painful, yet successful.

Comparatively, U.S. President Obama himself a devout socialist, continued spending post 2008 and is still spending at this writing (2016). In the wake of Bernanke's QE calamity against a backdrop of 50 million Americans on food stamps and more than 100 million on some form of government dole, the U.S. Dollar currency is being put into jeopardy of being devalued down to zero.

The current American meltdown is already showing signs of panic. Its neocon-liberalcon ideologs have been on a frantic campaign of diverting your attention by funding a catastrophic, public genocide, via a feverish "terrorphobia" campaign. If one puts an ear to the ground they will find that the financial tremors still persist before an impending earthquake; one which will clear its throat in historic proportions, unrivalled in recent history.

America's thirst for global resources seems to be draining the planet dry, with no ability to pay back what they use. The U.S. has been made a global addict to its finite resources. Being now bankrupt, the time is drawing near when it will make an attempt to shoot-the-dealer. Right now it preoccupies itself with only diverting public attention away from the facts that Washington, Israel, Turkey and Saudi Arabia, financed ISIS terrorists, while bombing 6,000 dud targets, paid for with taxpayer dollars, as it desperately seeks a fall guy.

American Socialists under Obama have pillaged the taxpayer's coffers to nearly dry. This careless mismanagement will cause great pains in rising interest rates. We know their death kneel is no longer distant, when government agencies are purchasing tanks and military equipment to be used on the streets of America with Operation Jade Helm being its stark reminder. The multipolar nations need to take a good look at these sinfully gross and barbaric atrocities to which this maddening unipolar, Zionist machine is resorting to. Israel is doing exactly what it said it would do; use the United States to cause misery to all non-Zionists, while reigning over a New World Order.

Martial law might very well be implemented, once interest rates skyrocket and cause consumables to become unaffordable. All entitlement programs and retirement accounts will be swung into jeopardy and there will likely be a "bank holiday" declared. This is where the banks will only disperse 50% of your balances, or less and keep the remainder. If an armed populace comes forth they might be profiled as terrorists, which would open up the door for possible gun confiscations. The IMF has already stated it plans to roll out a new currency in 2018, but we must remember we're dealing with "contingency freaks" here, so they have several alternate routes in chaos to choose from. They could suddenly pull the blanket out from under you and issue a "digital" currency instead.

A confiscation of precious metals and cash in exchange for "a new money" is another option too, not to mention the leasing of federal lands to gold mining corporations. Please don't forget that "The Men of Insanity" in the Foreign Policy Initiative are still living in a fantasy, blindly convinced that a nuclear war is "winnable". Zionist operatives in America's Industrial Military Complex are lobbying hard for a WW III, whether instigated by them, or false-flagged by one of their Zionist cell operatives. NATO positioning in Europe for this "end of all life" variable is being put into motion as you read this. This all has everything to do with why Bernanke is putting off the inevitable for as long as possible by purchasing $87 billion of U.S. debt per month. He can only execute these trades for a limited time period, before the fiscal reality of this equation wins.

"If" there is "a morning after" this will prove to be a eureka to the multipolar universe. It will reap an economic boom while the U.S. is imploding. Making up only 4% of the world's population, while consuming 30% of its resources, the U.S. will no longer be a parasite that the multipolar world will miss.

It will not be a pretty site in America for many generations and I would strongly suggest you keep your incorporating aspirations away from this Israeli colony. The Lavon Affair is their stenciled trademark, which can be found on everything they touch. The twin towers, Boston, Syria, California, Paris, they don't care; the trademark is always the same. Their desperation now constantly beats the drums for a concocted war with Russia. ABC, CBS, NBC, Fox and CNN; their Zionist drums always beat the loudest, but not a soldier will be found in their name. The world now stands cocked-and-ready, with all barrels aimed at the United States. It is a very broken and desperate hostage now, a place all should avoid for the rest of their lives.

..., getting back to that U.S. debt matter, have you ever wondered who owns The Federal Reserve? It's a privately owned bank whose shareholders are banks. The Honorable Louis McFadden, a once Chairman of the House Banking and Currency Committee, gave his assessment in 1930: "Some people think that the Federal Reserve Banks are United States Government institutions. They are private monopolies which prey upon the people of these United States for the benefit of themselves and their foreign customers; foreign and domestic speculators and swindlers and rich and predatory money lenders".

The Federal Reserve (or Fed) has acquired immense new powers recently. In an unheard of move in March 2008, the New York Fed advanced the funds for J.P. Morgan Chase to purchase investment bank Bear Sterns for pennies on the dollar. The deal was highly controversial (illegal) since Jamie Diamond, the CEO of J.P.

Morgan sits on the board of the New York Fed and was an active participant in the secret weekend negotiations.

In September 2008 the Federal Reserve did something even more profound; it purchased the world's largest insurance company. On September 16th the Fed announced it was granting an $85 billion loan to American International Group (AIG) for an 80% stake in the mega-insurer. The Associated Press coined it "a government takeover", but this was no ordinary reshuffling. The Treasury had already taken over Freddie Mac and Fannie Mae a week beforehand, but the Fed is not a government-owned agency. Equally astounding was the procedure for the way the deal was funded. Associated Press reported: "The Treasury Department, for the first time in history said it would begin selling bonds for the Federal Reserve in an effort to help the central bank deal with its unprecedented borrowing needs".

This was most bizarre (illegal). Why was the Treasury issuing U.S. Government bonds to fund the Federal Reserve, who was supposed to be "the lender of last resort" that was created to fund the banks and the federal government? Yahoo Finance reported on September 17th, "The Treasury is setting up a temporary financing program at the Fed's request. The program will auction Treasury bills to raise cash for the Fed's use. The initiative aims to help the Fed manage its balance sheets, following its effort to enhance its liquidity facilities over the previous few quarters".

In a normal world the Fed swaps green Federal Reserve Notes for pink pieces of paper called U.S. Bonds (U.S. Government I.O.U.'s), with the intent to provide Congress with funding it cannot raise through taxes. Now we have the government issuing bonds not for its own use, but for the Federal Reserve. It seems likely that this plan is actually swapping for the bank's toxic derivatives (illegally), without putting them up for sale.

According to Wikipedia, who make things more understandable than the Fed's own website: "The term Securities

Lending Facility is a 28 day facility which will offer Treasury general collateral to the Federal Reserve Bank of New York's primary dealers, in exchange for other program-eligible collateral. It is intended to promote liquidity in the financing markets for Treasury and other collateral and thus to foster the functioning of financial markets more generally. The resource allows dealers to switch debt that is less liquid for the U.S. government securities that are easily tradeable".

"To switch debt that is less liquid for U.S. government securities that are easily tradeable" would translate into the government getting the bank's toxic derivatives and the banks getting the government's AAA-securities. The Fed's website claims that this is not a private corporation, not ran for profit and isn't funded by Congress. Set up in 1913, the Federal Reserve served as "a lender of last resort" to stave off bank runs such as "The Panic of 1907". Its mandate was to assure the private banking system remain solvent. Simply put, that means preserving the system's most valuable assets; a "monopoly" on creating the national money supply. Aside from coins, each dollar circulating is now created privately as a debt to the Federal Reserve, or the banking system it oversees.

We can conclude that the Fed "is" privately owned. Private banks are 100% of its shareholders with none of its stock being owned by the U.S. government. The Fed does not receive "appropriations" from Congress, it receives money from Congress with no congressional approval by performing "open market operations". Wright Pitman, Chairman of the House Banking and Currency Committee in the 1960's once called the Federal Reserve "..., a total money-making machine. When the Federal Reserve writes a check for a government bond, it does exactly what any bank does, it creates money; it created money purely and simply by writing a check". On a regular basis, when the Fed guarantees its shareholders (private banks) to cover all operating expenses, plus a 6% return, this is a "for profit" corporation. Taxpayers pay $700 billion-a-year to banks in the U.S., all of which is completely unnecessary if only the Fed was eliminated and the government issued its own gold and silver-back money "interest free". Oh and by the way, did I fail to mention that "banks love war"!

Another piece to America's puzzle is in it having become an Israeli colony with Zionist operatives on Wall Street, in each of the six major media networks' top management, in the Federal Reserve, the U.S. Treasury and the Pentagon. You can see now why the cause for the American dilemma is found in the incubation and funding of terrorism, compounded by its "be afraid, be afraid" press and all having been controlled by the handlers (Zionist operatives) of its own government. Americans have been naively permitting this coup to run undeterred for the past 53 years.

Now on a much lighter and a bit less complicated (and law-biding) note; "Islamic Banking". It is consistent with the principles of "sharia law" (Islamic law). Islamic banking really means to be "compliant with sharia finance". It has become worthy of a serious look from the mainstream consumer and by that I mean "non-Muslims", as you do not have to be a Muslim to use Islamic banking services. Their conservative posturing has afforded these banks an extremely high reputation for being much more soundly financed and solvent. They also have a much higher degree of ethics, as just one a small example they do not provide services for entities connected with the pornography industry. And they are even considering expanding these ethics into the "environmentally friendly" universe.

A few examples of Islamic banks in the U.S. are Lariba's Bank of Whittier, California, Bank ABC of New York, Devon Bank of Chicago, UIF nationwide and Standard Charter, also available nationwide. Sharia prohibits acceptance of certain interest or fees for loans of money. Investments in companies supplying goods or services prohibited by Islamic principles, such as pork or alcohol are known as "haram" meaning sinful. These prohibiting factors have historically been applied in varying degrees in Muslims countries to safeguard Islamic practices.

In 2009 there were some 300 banks and 250 mutual funds who were sharia compliant. By 2014 sharia compliant total assets totaled $2 trillion. While many Zionist-Jewish bankers, brokers and news networks (ABC, CBS, NBC, Fox, and CNN) are busy trying to beat your head silly with hating and fearing Muslims, make sure to "keep an open mind". Remember that "ISIS" and "Islamic terrorists" were created for the most part, by Israelis and a handful of U.S. non-Muslim extremists. I would venture that 95% "of all people' just want to coexist peacefully and overlook our neighbor's differences. It is just a handful of very evil, Zionist-Jews and war profiteers who wish to constantly divide us.

In all honesty, Islamic banking deserves a second look. Though it only makes up a fraction of the banking assets of Muslims it is growing faster than any other banking assets. With an escalating annual rate of 18% from 2009-2013, it is forecast to grow an average of 20% annually to the year 2018. In 2009 the Vatican put forward the idea that "the principles of Islamic finance may represent a possible cure for ailing markets". The Catholic Church used to forbid usury (unnecessary interest and fees on money loans), but relaxed its ban in the 16th century.

The common requirements of Islamic banking are based on "risk sharing" which is a part of trade and not risk-transfer. Islamic banking offers concepts such as "profit sharing" (Mudharaba), "safekeeping" (Wadiah), "joint venture" (Musharakah), "costs plus" (Murabahah) and "leasing" (Ijar). It excludes any transactions related to alcohol, pork, gambling, pornography, etc. Its goal is to be involved in only ethical investing and moral purchases.

Other domestic alternatives for Westerners seeking sounder choices in banks might also consider Bank of India and Bank of China. Offhand, I know of a Bank of India in San Francisco and the Bank of China-New York in the U.S. For other ex-U.S. investments there are also American Depository Receipts (ADRs), which are securities in foreign corporations, but are backed by the currency of their country-specific location and "not" in U.S. dollars.

Banking and finance ministers at the 7th World Islamic Retail Banking Conference (WIRBC), met in November of 2015. An important tone was set in some of its following statements: "The reality of today's world is that social media, peer-to-peer transactions and crowdfunding are real phenomenon. Digitization is the future of Islamic banking. Parallel industries like Paypal, Facebook and Google are all getting into finance. Instead of looking at them as only a threat we should look at them as an opportunity in a collaborative world. We as bankers can't afford to close our eyes anymore. There are threats as well as opportunities out there".

Rajashekara Maiya, associated vice-president and global head of Project and Strategy Presales at Infosys Finacle noted, that the world had changed and that digitally enabled players are disrupting banking. He also added that digitization is the future of Islamic Banking and that it was important to have a customer-centric approach. "The customer", he said, "is the focal point of the business. Options are many and loyalty is limited. Convenience, speed and personalization are all needed, since customers today seek partners, not providers. The future lies in opening up your bank".

Speaking on the importance of bank branches in regions, Shaker Zainal, regional head of distribution at Mashreq said that, "based on recent research, a customer visits a branch three times-a-year on average. People like branches because they trust them. Branches today still matter and are critical to attracting new customers. Sixty percent of potential customers will not stop to consider you if you don't have a branch." When dealing with customers, he noted that it is important to focus on "instant fulfillment" as well as on relationships and customer engagement outside of the bank branches. The world is now awakening to both a willingness and a need for Islamic Banking to become a much more acceptable alternative in the mainstream banking landscape of today. Potential customers need to become more aware of the many important services and advantages Islamic Banking may be able to offer them, not just for Muslims, but for all consumers.

An example of the rapid, economic growth of the multipolar world's Muslim countries is Iran. A case in point would be an Iranian corporation known as Iran Khodro (IKCO), where innovation has always played a key role. It is the leading Iranian vehicle maker, headquartered in Tehran. Its original name was Iran National. Having been founded in 1962, it put out some 688,000 automobiles in 2009. IKCO manufactures vehicles for Sammand, Peugot and Renault cars, trucks, minibuses and buses. Iran Khodro was founded by Ahmad Khayami. The word "khodro" means "automobile" in Persian.

Iran Khodro Industrial Group (IKCOOS) is a public joint-stock company. Its aim is to create and manage factories for the manufacturing of assorted types of vehicles and parts, as well as selling and exporting them. It produces vehicles for more than 13 separate brands and has become the largest vehicle manufacturer in the Middle East, Central Asia and North Africa. It is the largest vehicle manufacturer in Iran, with some 65% of the vehicle production market.

For more than 30 years Iran Khodro produced the Paykan, a car developed by the Rootes Group's Root Arrow range, best known as the "Hillman Hunter". The firm has long-term relationships with EU and Asian manufacturers such as PSA Peugot, Citroen, Renault,

Mercedes-Dailmer Benz, Suzuki and soon, Italy wishes to initiate a partnership.

With both the lifting of Iran sanctions and the reconciliation with PSA Peugot Citroen, Iran Khodro is posed well for explosive growth. Its true test of time will be how well it will adapt to its regional markets, once "more green" and "full electric" vehicles become popular with its local consumers. Recently German, French and Italian trade delegations have been frequenting Iran Khodro facilities, with some historic deals being solidified and new win-win, long-term contracts.

Iran Khodro has managed to capture the majority of the Iraq market, something its competitors have failed to achieve. Sammand Peugot Pars and the Peugot 405 are among the main Iranian vehicles being produced in neighboring Iraq and soon, another model the Arisan will also be joining that list as well. Iraqis prefer to purchase Iranian vehicles for their good quality and easy, prompt, after sales services.

Iran is the Middle East's largest automobile market with auto-manufacturing being the country's largest industry after oil. Iran's auto market is on track to averaging more than 1.7 million sedans in annual sales. Manufacturers from Germany, Italy, France and S. Korea are negotiating to get footholds there and already the competition is intensifying for a share of the upside potentials.

Another Muslim country proving valuable to the BRICS countries' promising growth and opportunities is Pakistan. Pakistan Telecommunication Company Ltd (PTCL) is the chief telecommunications authority in Pakistan. The company is a telephone and internet provider with services nationwide and is the backbone for Pakistan's digital infrastructure, despite an influx of competition from names like Telenor Corp and China Mobile. The company oversees some 2,000 exchanges and supplies the largest fixed-line network. Data and other services such as GSM, CDMA,

IPTV, broadband internet and wholesale are all increasing parts of the business.

Creating opportunities - Enabling people
PTCL's 1 year internship program
A Year Can Define Your Future!

Under an intensified program for privatization in 2006, initiated by Prime Minister Shaukat Aziz, 26% of PTCL was sold to Etisalat telecommunications with 12% becoming publically held. Sixty-two percent still remains government, state owned. Shortly following the Abu Dhabi-based company's Etisalat and public offering as partial owners in PTCL, it was not welcomed in all circles. Countrywide protests ensued and strikes were held by PTCL workers. They destabilized phone lines to many institutions such as Punjab University, with many services becoming blocked. The military was forced to overtake the management of all exchanges nationwide. Many workers were arrested and jailed. The disagreements between the government and employees finally ended with a 30% increase in workers' salaries.

In addition to being Pakistan's largest telecommunications entity, PTCL is also the largest CDMA operator, while maintaining a leading presence as an influential infrastructure provider to other corporate clients and telecom operators. It seems well positioned to be a vital agent in Pakistan's economic growth. Though PTCL's corporate culture is still in its infancy of development, its structure is beginning to take shape. In discussions are rewards and motivational incentives, as well as concepts for better performance tracking, less resistance in communications between workers and middle management, increased accountability for government owned sectors in management, better uniformity in manager practices and dispositions and the possibility for improved investments in worker education programs.

In addition to its wire-line services, PTCL also provides fixed line services through its CDMA based Wireless Local Loop (WLL) network with its VFone brand. The company provides fixed broadband through conventional copper wire and FTTC wireless broadband through its brand name EVO. Its cellular division remains the second largest in Pakistan through the Ufone subsidiary. PTCL also offers some of the world's first commercial HDTV services based on IPTV with the brand name SmartTV, as well as home surveillance and alarm capabilities over broadband, under the name iSentry. In addition, PTCL remains part of the consortium for three major submarine communications cable networks and has laid on-land Optical Fiber Access Network in Pakistan's major metropolitan cities. Local loop services are being modernized and upgraded from copper to an optical network.

Keeping in step with Pakistan's larger global perspective, PTCL's Long Distance and international infrastructure is expanding the capacity in two of its SEA-ME-WE submarine cable systems, to meet the increasing demands of its nation's international traffic.

Chapter   Three

The Day America Died; Empires in Decline

In 1947 John Kennedy first arrived on the scene at Capitol Hill. He was the son of a very wealthy man, an icon in American finance. This very rich man, his father Joseph P. Kennedy reaped millions from the stock market in both directions during the Roaring 20's, not to mention from a hushed stint in smuggling booze across the Canadian border during prohibition. Franklin D. Roosevelt appointed Joe Kennedy Chairman of the new Securities and Exchange Commission. It was no secret in Washington that the ambassador had awarded John and his other 8 siblings their own million dollar trust funds. It was a common assumption that his dad had bought his seat in Congress with sizeable campaign funds. And so it was for a few years, after Jack appeared in Congress he appeared as nothing more than just another rich man's son.

Following an historic upset which skyrocketed him to the presidency, he introduced pioneering phrase and verse into economic theory. He debated that "tax cuts" would stimulate the economy and that the idea of a balanced budget was a misleading mythology. Following the 1961 Recession there was a need to get money into the economy fast. And no one will deny that Jack's brilliance accomplished just that. He instructed all Federal agencies to accelerate their procurements and construction. Kennedy then released more than $1 billion in State Highway aid ahead of schedule. He then raised farm price supports and advanced their pay, while speeding up the distribution of tax refunds and GI life insurance dividends. He initiated a Food Stamp program for the needy and increased the number of U.S. Employment Offices. Jack then encouraged the Federal Reserve Board to keep long-term interest rates low, by buying long-term bonds.

During Kennedy's first four years as president, the United States experienced the strongest and longest case of economic expansion in the nation's history. GDP alone rose more in 4 years, than it had during the previous 8. By 1964 a record $100 billion and 16% growth in the nation's output provided over 2.75 million more jobs and a record rise in labor income. Idle manufacturing capacity was cut in half and for the first time the 70-million jobs barrier had been shattered. By the last quarter of 1963, the investment tax credit and liberalized depreciation allowances encouraged investment.

Kennedy's policies had resulted in the longest American peacetime expansion of the economy in the century of recorded business cycle history. The rise in the gross domestic product was 5.6%-a-year, while profits, wages and salaries were higher than ever before. Non-agriculture employment added more than a million jobs, the average factory work week blew past 40 hours and the economy raced to new records in consumer spending, labor income and industrial production.

In the time leading up to the president's death, four paramount elements would eventually foster a quadruple arch rivalry. These four adversaries were:

1: Israel

2: The Industrial Military Complex

3: The keepers of the "elite aircrafts" (otherwise known as U.F.O.'s)

4: The Federal Reserve

Both outgoing President Eisenhower and Kennedy shared two similarities, across party lines. Both distrusted Israel and both were wary of a surmounting military machine which was beginning to go to bed with Wall Street. The genius in Kennedy as president had made plans early on, to nip all four in the bud. His fatal mistake was he did not construct a solid enough infrastructure inside his personal security, his partnerships and his allies, to withstand the blowback of a four dimension giant. It is within the fundamentals of this most historic scenario of the 20th century which gave cause to the exact time-of-death for the American democracy.

Focusing on Jack's intentions he:

1: Threatened to cut off aid to Israel, if it could not allow US weapons inspectors' entry and prove it was not secretly building nuclear weapons in Dimona.

2: Began drawing up plans to have all American troops be withdrawn from Vietnam by 1965.

3: Warned Naval Intelligence he was going to issue an ultimatum to reveal and share with the American people the existence of highly advanced aircrafts (U.F.O.'s) in their possession which were reverse-engineered from the inherited technology of Third Reich scientists.

4: Intended to completely phase-out the Federal Reserve by issuing U.S. dollars backed by silver.

This is not "conspiracy theorizing", this is exploring and interpreting actual American history. It is important to make the world aware that most American's haven't realized that their democracy now exists only in a dream. It is of equal importance for all nations to understand the causes for American democracy's death, so that they may gain vital insight into ways they can better protect themselves, their sovereignty and prosperity.

Before exploring the detailed causes, an introductory outline covering the events is as follows:

The W.A.S.P. flank (White Anglo-Saxon Protestant) of the U.S. Industrial Military Complex had no intentions of power-sharing. It cut Israel in on the deal of assassinating Kennedy for the stakes of continuing aid to Israel and also to turn a blind eye to its nuclear aspirations only.

The keepers of the elite aircrafts were multinational elitists. Their only involvement was in reaffirming the preservation of their anonymity. The Fed on the other hand, had already been in bed with the Israelis since its inception as a nation. So within the crime scene which followed there actually was "a double assassination". The elitists from their aircrafts played the role as innocent bystanders. The "WASP shark" then consumed Kennedy while the Fed rode an even bigger fish, the "Israeli shark" which gobbled up the WASP shark and made them all guppies in a fish bowl.

As closely accurate as can be interpreted from the mountains of evidence, Mossad-CIA operatives, in conjunction with William Greer the Secret Service driver of Kennedy's Dallas limo, put the plot into motion. Small in caliber, the first shots were fired from the "grassy knoll" hitting the president in the throat. This caused him to grasp his collar and tilt his head slightly backwards. The killing shot was fired by a specially designed, high-powered air-pistol, its ammo being exploding bullet-heads which were heavily laced with shellfish toxins.

For 16 years William Cooper, a former Naval Intelligence officer turned whistleblower, searched for video coverage of the assassination which included the driver. All major U.S. News media cut out that portion of the scene and anyone possessing such copies had them confiscated. Finally Cooper uncovered a copy showing in startling detail, William Greer delivering the killing shot. It was aired on a Salt Lake City news network, with Bill Cooper narrating and can still be found on YouTube (at least, at this writing). It is also the reason the president's wife Jacqueline, was desperately trying to climb out of the limo over the top of the trunk.

In 1960 the clash began. Outgoing president Eisenhower's administration sought an explanation for secretive construction near Dimona in Israel. The U.S. was told this top secret activity in the middle of the desert was purely a textile mill. It was also told it was not allowed to visit this site. Classified surveillance photos then appeared on the front page of The New York Times.

Once Jack took the office of president in 1961 this issue became a major crisis. Kennedy was neither hostile nor sympathetic towards the Israelis. His advisers encouraged continued pressure for inspections assuming Israel would have no choice. For two years Ben Gurion avoided the issues by dancing around them. Finally President Kennedy drew his line in the sand. On May 18, 1963 he sent a personal letter to Israel's Prime Minister Gurion warning, that unless U.S. weapons inspectors were permitted into the Dimona facility Israel would find itself totally isolated.

Soon after, the "last American president with guts and a backbone" was gunned down in Dallas. And no following administration has ever done anything more than cower, write checks and bow on bended knee to Israel, while continuing unabated to take orders from this terrorist state.

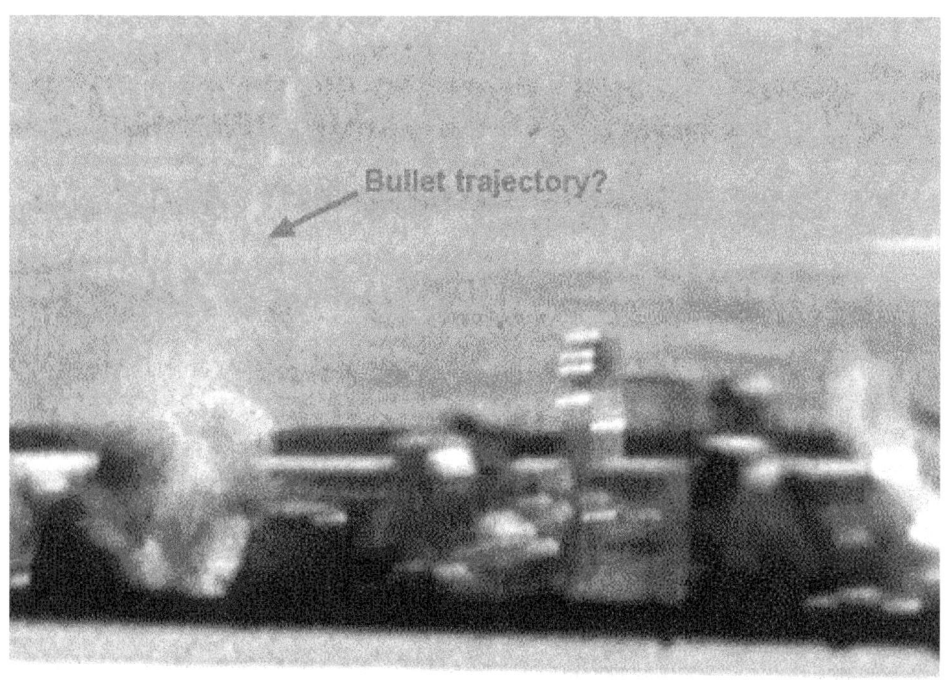

Bullet trajectory?

(Trajectory line follows throat shot. Greer has just discharged the head shot)

Now from the Federal Reserve's angle leading up to Jack's assassination, I've uncovered the following interpreted notes of the late Boylston Street, Boston lawyer, J.P. Curran esq., 1970:

On June 4th, 1963 a virtually unknown Presidential decree (Executive Order) was signed with the authority to strip the Federal Reserve Bank of its power to loan money to the United States. It is with the greatest of irony that this is exactly what the multipolar nations of today are in the process of doing to the IMF and World Bank, as well as the U.S. dollar as a reserve currency.

With the stroke of a pen, President Kennedy declared that the privately owned Federal Reserve Bank would soon be out of business. The Christian Law Fellowship exhaustively researched this through the Federal Register and Library of Congress. It was safely concluded that this Executive Order has never been repealed, amended, or superceded by any subsequent Executive Order. In other words, it is still valid.

When President John Fitzgerald Kennedy – author of "Profile in Courage" – signed this Order it returned to the Treasury Department, the Constitutional power to create and issue money without going through the privately owned Fed. Kennedy's Executive Order gave the Treasury Department the explicit authority: "to issue silver certificates against any bullion, silver, or standard silver dollars in the Treasury". This meant that for every ounce of silver in the U.S. Treasury's vault, the government could introduce new currency into circulation, based on the silver bullion based there. As a result, more than $4 billion in the United States Notes were brought into circulation in $2 and $5 denominations. $10 and $20 Notes were never circulated, but were being printed by the Treasury Department when Kennedy was assassinated.

"United States Notes" were issued as an "interest-free", "debt-free" currency backed by silver reserves in the U.S. Treasury. When one compares a "Federal Reserve Note" issued by the Fed with Kennedy's U.S. Treasury issued "United States Note" they almost appear identical, only the Fed's notes were with a green seal and the

U.S. note had a red seal. U.S. Notes also read at the bottom, "redeemable in silver" on them.

The president was assassinated on November 22, 1963. The United States notes he had issued were immediately taken out of circulation. I can remember having several of these $2 notes when I was a boy. We used to call them "silver certificates" and Thomas Jefferson's portrait was on them. According to the United States Secret Service, 99% of all U.S. paper currency circulating in 1999 were Federal Reserve Notes.

Kennedy was well aware that if the silver-backed United States Notes were widely circulated they would have removed the need for the Federal Reserve Notes. This is not only a very simple matter of economics, but of fiscal and ethical responsibility, as well as more a "moral act of courage". Kennedy's actions challenged the powers behind the Federal Reserve's dominance over money creation and world finance. He had boldly faced the two most successful instruments that ever were used to increase debt: 1) War (Vietnam) and 2) The creation of money by a privately owned central bank. In his efforts to have all troops out of Vietnam by 1965, combined with the Executive Order would have shattered the profits and control of the private Federal Reserve.

The United States notes were backed by silver, while the Federal Reserve Notes were backed by nothing more than intrinsic value. The president's Executive Order would have prevented the national debt from reaching its trillion dollar elevations. If LBJ or any following, standing president were to maintain Kennedy's Order it would have literally eliminated all of the $9 trillion in government deficits of that historic era. It would have then cost the United States Government "nothing" to create money because it would no longer need the Fed to do so.

The shear and profound cowardice of America to demonstrate "no push-back" whatsoever, no objections, no raising of questions, no oversight with no protest into the Kennedy assassination is what surrendered their democracy to a silent coup d' et tat and pronounced it dead-on-arrival in perpetuity. In short, the United States of America only lasted 187 years (1776-1963) and has been operating under "a completely new regime, for the past 53 years" (1963-2016)! The regime that killed the country's last, authentic American president.

Now perpetual war can continue unabated, Israel's control power which infiltrated and permeated rapidly throughout the system like a pandemic virus is approaching a total consumption of the host; its fingers now positioned on all the nuclear triggers. The profits of the Federal Reserve's blood monies have now compounded into infinity, while industrial production has all been exported. And all this now stands against a backdrop of an Industrial Military Complex's uninterrupted quests for murder, mayhem and destruction before a horizon blacked with an endless tide of armored tanks and weaponry.

For the past 53 years the United States democracy has only truly existed in the dream world, not in reality. Thanks to the cowardice silence and surrender of its citizenry and the symbolic ineptitude in its politicians, it remains nothing more than a conquered, raped, psychotic, debt-ridden killing machine. It is the epitome of liberal totalitarianism in a final pollination before a Zionist-fascist harvest. However much longer it will take, the day will eventually arrive, just as it did for those 66 million tortured and executed Russians, where many people in this country will die on their own nation's soil.

Executive Order 11110:

AMENDMENT OF EXECUTIVE ORDER NO# 10289 AS AMENDED, RELATING TO THE PERFORMANCE OF CERTAIN FUNCTIONS AFFECTING THE DEPARTMENT OF THE TREASURY. By virtue of the authority vested in me by section 301 of title 3 of the United States Code, it is ordered as follows: SECTION1. Executive Order 10289 of September 19, 1951, as amended, is hereby further amended-a) By adding at the end of paragraph 1 thereof the following subparagraph (j): "(j) The authority vested in the President by paragraph (b) of section 43 of the Act of May 12, 1933, as amended (31 U.S.C. 821 (b), to issue silver certificates against any silver bullion, silver, or standing silver dollars of the Treasury not then held for redemption of any outstanding silver certificates, to prescribe the denominations of such silver certificates, and to coin standard silver dollars and subsidiary silver currency for their redemption," and (b) By revoking subparagraphs (b) and (c) of paragraph 2 thereof. SECTION 2. The amendment made by this Order shall not affect any act done, or any right accruing or accrued or any suit or proceeding had or commenced in any civil or criminal cause prior to the date of this Order, but all liabilities shall continue and may be enforced as if said amendments, had not been made.

The concept of producing a different type of energy for a revolutionary, never before conceived type of aircraft first began to take shape in 1917. This project started in Germany and was initially fully funded by both secretive organizations of the Thule and Vril societies. During the beginning of 20th century, under the Third Reich's development and rise, Germany became home to a wide assortment of wealthy occult groups. Some of these were built upon purely theoretical beliefs and concepts of social and government orders, while others were known for their more concentrated focus of incorporating a "New Science" into their platforms. The chances highly favor that Victor Schauberger could be said to be "The Father of U.F.O.s", or at least the individual being responsible for enabling the theory of such a craft to gain its first traction for enabling them to come into actual production. His prototype worked on the principal of levitation, implosion and anti-matter.

(Actual photo of an RSB-2 in flight)

In 1934 the Vril society produced the very first production of the world's first craft of this nature, the RSB-2. It was saucer-shaped and extended some 16 feet in diameter. Its first successful flight emitted different hues of the colors red, orange, yellow, green, white, blue and violet, depending on the amount of power applied.

This technology remained highly under wraps until it caught the attention of Hitler's "Black Sun" research and development division, known as SS-IV. By 1939 they built their own similar craft called the RSB-5. It was the very first long distance craft of this new technology, measuring more than 65 feet across and was known as "Haunebu-1".

For some seventy years Schauberger aircrafts have existed and are in production (however low), here on planet Earth. President Kennedy was aware of this knowledge and intended to break their shroud of silence and supported having this technology be incorporated into all of American society, not just to remain reserved for an elite group of secret organizations and individuals.

In one of the late William Cooper's interviews the former Naval Intelligence officer not only described his accounts in detail of actually encountering these crafts in operation, but the elite's reason for keeping them secret. Not only do they enable "a very few" to set up alternative living arrangements off-planet, but they also serve as "a contingency" for elite globalists whereby they may at any given time stage a "false-flag invasion from space" and forcing Earth's inhabitants to unite under one rule, which of course they will stand to control and benefit from the most. Yes, just another New World Order contingency plan, nothing more.

(Computer generated image of an RSB-5)

Created by the insatiable greed and bottomless appetite of elitists in the first place, the planet's atmosphere now spins terminally damaged and irreparable. While the very ones who profited most from it, will be venturing off to live in other worlds. The Earth has been pushed too far; to a point in time that has set its own self-healing process into motion. The future should prove to be anything but boring. I hold out hope for many a human hat trick in the wings.

Babylonians, Assyrians, Romans, Greeks and other civilizations were great super powers that all rose to great heights of development and fell. After the 25th Dynasty the Egyptians suffered a fall of epic proportions. Between 1776-1788 Edward Gibbons' "The History of the Decline and Fall of the Roman Empire" was published in six huge volumes. His immense scholarly aspirations finely included a period in history stretching some 1,200 years. His objectives were to meticulously account the elements which gave cause to the Empire's rise, as well as how a robust and energized one could be sabotaged and destabilized. He appears to allude to a conclusion that "luxury" breeds a fraudulent synthesis to its DNA.

There are various contributing factors to the Roman Empire's fall. One each interconnected to the next. Some agree that Christianity transformed Rome's citizenry into peace activism, creating problems in their defense against invading barbarians. They claimed the revenues used to build churches might have been put to better use in the upkeep of their municipalities.

On the flip side of the coin, others claim a convincing rebuttal that Christianity was responsible for fortifying the Empire's moral and ethical fabric of its foundation and actually helped to prolong its existence. These debatable proceedings are still being discussed to this day. Gibbons mentioned some eight basic causes for the Roman Empire's extinction. In a comparison to say a United States of today, one might attempt to determine just how much is evolving organically vs how much might be instilling the contributing elements with viral intentions.

1: <u>Decline in Morals and Values</u>: The morals and values which solidified the legions of Rome became undone near the end of the empire. Decadence directly began trickling down from affluence. A belligerent disregard for human life manifested itself in the gladiator games and the divorce, crime and prostitution rates increased.

2: <u>Public Health</u>: Public health and environmental problems were widespread in the empire's later stages. This segment is unique to Rome, in that it possessed two outstanding factors; the wealthy's foolhardy affinity for lead-pipe plumbing and a high rate of spilt blood and carnage at the gladiator games.

3: <u>Political Corruption</u>: The Romans it seemed, were always lacking in developing a viable and direct process for choosing a new Emperor. It was open to debate which included the army, the Praetorian Guard (emperor's private army), the Senate and the old emperor. Over time, the Praetorian Guard took absolute authority to decide and they were rewarded handsomely in the final process.

In 186 A.D. the army strangled the emperor and a practice of selling the throne to the highest bidder became practice. During the next 100 years, Rome had 37 different emperors, 25 of whom were assassinated.

4: <u>Unemployment</u>: Towards the last quarter of the empire's reign, farming was located on large estates known as latifundias, which were owned by wealthy men using slave labor. Most farmers could not compete with the prevailing low commodity prices of the day and were forced to sell their farms. They then joined the ranks of the unemployed in inner cities, which in turn exasperated the crime rate. Eventually the emperor was forced to import grain to feed its poor, some 100,000 in Rome alone.

5: <u>Inflation</u>: Increases in taxes inhibited the stability and health of the economy. Tax collections were needed to fund government deficits, food for the people and government sponsored diversion functions, such as circuses and sporting events. As the final days of Rome grew closer, a much greater emphasis was placed around sports games to divert attention away from the malignant cancer which was quietly spreading throughout its internal apparatus. It was following the reign of Marcus Aurelius that the Roman Empire's economy started to buckle under from inflation. Their conquest over new territories drew to a crawl, causing the influx of gold into the economy to dwindle.

Still, high amounts of gold continued to be paid for luxury items, while it meant less gold available for coining currency. As the percentage of gold used in coins went down, it decreased their value. To compensate for this the merchants raised prices. Inevitably, more people began to resorting to barter over actual currency. This contagion finally led to salaries having to be paid in food and clothing and the collection of taxes actual fell to the level of being exchanged with fruits and vegetables.

6: <u>Urban Decay</u>: Affluent Romans saw their homes adorned with marble walls and floors, fancy colored tiles and colorful glass windows. However, most of the empire's citizens were now poor. The middle-class appeared nearly non-existent, which found the bulk of society living in vile, efficiency-like apartments averaging six stories. Each complex covered an entire city block and there was an estimated 44,000 such apartment houses within Rome's city walls at one time. First floor apartments were the most expensive, while the upper floors were rented by the poor. These rickety flats always emitted a vile odor and the higher up one lived, the cheaper the rent became.

The flats often experienced stifling temperatures and became filthy, overcrowded and unsafe. Anyone who could not pay was forced to live on crime infested streets. Under these conditions the inner city began to decay.

7: Inferior Technology: The last 400 years of the Roman Empire witnessed great scientific and engineering achievements, yet the empire's technologies grew too limited. Though it built impressive roads, bridges and aqueducts, they invented few machines for increasing productivity and efficiency. They could not manufacture enough goods for their own growing population. Conquering grew to a standstill and the land mass of the empire began to shrink.

8: Military Spending: The upkeep of an army to protect the empire against invading barbarians became a chronic bane to the government. Much of the revenues needed for public housing and municipal routine maintenance gravitated increasingly into defense. Many infuriated Romans began losing their commitment to protect the empire. The government found itself recruiting soldiers from unemployed mobs or foreign countries. An army of this nature proved to be both unreliable and expensive. This forced emperors to raise taxes more often, which would eventually give further rise to inflation.

If you recall in the second chapter, Glubb Pasha narrowed his interpretations down to seven stages of great empires; pioneering, conquest, commerce, affluence, intellect, decadence and decline.

Both Glubb and Gibbons' accounts, though different in theory seem to cross paths in an agreement involving "the fourth stage". Glubb titled his "affluence" and Gibbons called his fourth stage "unemployment", which is indirectly the same, since the unemployment he refers to, was largely caused by affluent men who controlled all the farms with slave labor.

What both men's findings seem to be saying is that once "commerce" arrives on the scene, things begin to change. Larger amounts of money begin to change hands more frequently, which eventually lets "corruption" in the door where "affluence" is soon to follow.

So how do we intervene and block this cycle from taking place? Two things which might come to mind could be "subdividing" and "limiting wealth". My solution; the generation which follows a "commercial" one (meaning, the first generation of affluence) should leave the empire to pioneer and conquest for enough land, resources and savings for their own generation and the following. This isn't to be taken in the literal sense, but the "pioneering" and "conquest" stages could be "peacefully" repeated in some form of hybridization, on the outskirts of the existing civilization.

It is history's undeniable proof that "too much wealth, affluence and luxury" is the root of all evil in every society. It is a grotesque hijacking of fairness and balance in wealth distribution. Had this stage been purposely interrupted with my solution, there would have been thriving small farmers and more than enough revenues to go around for all of Rome's budgetary shortfalls, by rechanneling the excesses of wealth "back into the society" and not the pockets of a privileged few. Just imagine what the U.K. could be like if its royal family had to surrender 80% of its wealth and pump it back into the society. Every pupil in Britain would be going to school with their own laptops on clean, crime-free streets where everyone had a job! However, somewhere in the equation individuals would still have to come forth and inspire the culture with a sense of true "innovation". I concur this would have taken place in Rome had there only been a much more prevalent and thriving middle class.

America unfortunately, is on a fixed track to hell because its handlers shall always refuse having things any other way. There is however, the greatest chances for trying some of these new economic models in much younger, smaller and more open-minded societies, which can be found throughout the multipolar universe.

Since the fall of the American democracy, its Industrial Military Complex seems to have been burgeoning unfettered. Perhaps it can be said that it all started by the planting of just one tiny seed. The variety of that seed was likely of the genius "deception" and the location of its plantation was known as "The Gulf of Tonkin". Its planter was U.S. Secretary of Defense, Robert McNamara.

If you see a war and you watch the war and you begin to provide intelligence to one side in the war, then you have just invited yourself to be at war. War is hell, plain and simple. And it doesn't wait to send out formal invitations. Screaming "he shot at me first" has no bearing. After all, you invited yourself to be shot at.

In 1964 the U.S. backed and supported covert South Vietnamese commando raids conducted intelligence collecting operations along the North Vietnam coastline. The mission's code name was often referred to as OPLAN 34A, its objective and itinerary were devised and presided over by the U.S. Department of Defense, in conjunction with the CIA. The blood and guts of the operation was conducted by the South Vietnamese Navy.

Numerous South Vietnamese were captured and many OPLN 34 fighters suffered large casualties. By July of 1964 Lt. General William Westmoreland changed the objective's maneuvers to shore bombing with mortars, rockets and rifle fire from only South Vietnamese patrol boats.

During this time the U.S. Navy had been orchestrating reconnaissance and SIGINT-gathering operations further out from shore in the Tonkin Gulf. Destroyers conducted these so-called Desoto missions. A top-secret document declassified in 2005 listed the standing orders of the Desoto missions: "Locate and identify all coastal radar transmitters, note all navigational aids along the DRV's (Democratic Republic of Vietnam) coastline and monitor the Vietnamese junk fleet for a possible connection to DRV/Viet Cong maritime supply and infiltration of supply routes".

One should keep in mind that these operations involved the same CIA (1961-1966) which totally botched Kennedy's Cuba invasion at the "Bay of Pigs" by sending the troops the wrong size ammunition for their rifles. It was an international embarrassment, causing defeat and a large loss of life unnecessarily!

The United States was playing a dangerous game. The South Vietnamese, in carrying out OPLAN 34A attacks while using U.S. Navy support and collaboration against North Vietnam targets meant to some arguably, that the U.S. was taking it upon itself to fight someone else's war.

On July 28, 1964 the USS Maddox a DD-731 destroyer sortied out from Taiwan to voyage on a Desoto patrol. It was specially outfitted with a communications intercept van and 17 SIGINT technicians. The Maddox was to patrol in international waters off the North Vietnamese coastline, between the demilitarized zone (the DMZ) and the China-Vietnam border. On the night of July 30-31 the Maddox was on a station in the Gulf of Tonkin when a 34A attack was launched against Hon Me Island. With two boats, South Vietnamese raiders used machine guns and small cannon fire to attack the island radar and military installations. Simultaneously, two other South Vietnamese commando boats staged a similar attack against Hon Ngu Island, over twenty-five miles to the south.

After observing North Vietnamese torpedo vessels pursuing the South Vietnamese boats the Maddox withdrew from the area. When later queried by NSA headquarters the Maddox indicated it was unaware of the 34A attack on the island. This situation forced an eventual showdown between North Vietnam and U.S. Navy intelligence gathering missions.

On August 1st the Maddox returned to the same vicinity and began patrol. In the early morning of August 2nd Maddox communications specialists netted SIGINT reports that that North Vietnamese vessels were in route to the area, possibly to attack it. The onboard ship commander, Captain John Herrick ordered the Maddox out to sea, in the hopes to avoid a confrontation. However, at 10:45 he reversed those orders turning the Maddox back towards the coast, only this time north of the Hon Me Island.

The weather was clear, the waters calm. At 1440 hours, the destroyer discovered three North Vietnamese patrol boats gaining on it from the west. Captain Herrick then ordered Maddox gun crews to open fire if the quickly approaching vessels closed to within 10,000 yards. At 1505 hours three 5 inch shots were fired across the bow of the nearest vessel. In response, the leading vessel launched a torpedo and turned away. The first 5" shot fired from the Maddox would later be known as "the first shot fired in the U.S.-Vietnam War".

The second of the three vessels then launched two additional torpedoes and was then hit by gunfire from the Maddox. The first boat which turned away began to re-engage, launching its second torpedo and opening firing with its 14.5mm guns, but the Maddox shell fire heavily damaged this vessel.

Meanwhile overhead, four F-8 Crusaders from the USS Ticonderoga (CVA14) began swiftly approaching. Navy Commander James Stockdale, one of the pilots recalls that they flew over an untouched Maddox at 1530 hours, just minutes past the 22 minute surface battle had ended. He cited all enemy vessels were heading northwest at 40 knots, with two in front and the third lingering about a mile behind. The Maddox was seen retiring to the south.

The F-8 pilots had orders to attack and destroy and made multiple firing runs on the enemy vessels. The two lead boats began to zig-zag, but were hit heavily regardless. The third was left dead in the water burning. The following day the Maddox continued its Desoto patrols, it was said, "to demonstrate American resolve and its right to navigate in international waters". President Johnson then ordered the USS Turner Joy (DD-951) to join the Maddox on patrol.

On the morning of August 4th, U.S. intelligence was reporting that the North Vietnamese were planning to conduct offensive navy maneuvers in the Gulf of Tonkin. The clear conditions of the last two days had given way to rain torrents and thunderstorms, with poor visibility and six foot waves. On top of these difficult conditions for detection, the Maddox's SPS-40 long range radar and the Turner Joy's SPG-53 fire control radar were deemed inoperable. That night the Maddox's Captain Herrick ordered both ships out to sea.

Nonetheless, the Maddox at 2040 hours reported it was tracking unknown vessels, even though the destroyers were cruising at some 100 miles from shore, the approaching boats appeared to come at the ships from multiple directions. It was reported that some would appear, disappear, and then reappear from a different direction. There was an assumption that these reported vessels demonstrated maneuvering dispositions identical to torpedo boats.

Over the next three hours the two destroyers sailed at high speeds to avoid detection. The destroyers reported over twenty torpedo attacks, automatic weapons fire, enemy cockpit lights, torpedo wakes, various surface and air contacts and search light illumination. By the time both destroyers had ended their counter attack, they had fired five depth charges, 123 three inch shells and 249 five inch shells.

F-8 fighter pilot Commander Stockdale would again reappear in this scene. His wingman's craft had developed mechanical issues, but Stockdale managed to obtain permission to fly solo from the Ticonderoga. He was sighted over the Maddox at 2135 hours. For more than 90 minutes he conducted runs along both destroyers' course below 2,000 feet, searching for the enemy vessels. He later reported, "I had the best seat in the house to watch that event and our destroyers were just shooting at phantom targets – there were no PT boats there…, there was nothing there, but black water and American firepower".

The Maddox's Captain Herrick started to have his doubts about the attacks. While the battle continued he realized they were more likely due to the results of "overeager sonar technicians" and questionable equipment performance. During the entire "so-called" event the Turner Joy hadn't detected a single torpedo. At one point the Maddox Captain concluded that its operators were probably misled by the ship's own propellers reflecting off the rudder while in sharp turns. The destroyers head gun director was never able to lock onto any suspected targets since he became more inclined to interrupt that his radar was only picking up the activity of stormy seas' wave tops.

On August 5th at 0127 hours the Maddox Captain questioned his crew and analyzed the proceeding hours of the event, which now seemed to have more issues than answers. He sent a "highest priority" flash message to Honolulu. Declaring his doubts, he sent: "Review of action makes many reported contacts and torpedoes fired seem doubtful. Freak weather effects and overeager sonar personnel have accounted for many reports. No actual, visual sighting by Maddox. Suggest complete evaluation before further action taken".

Messages declassified in 2005 and from recently released tapes from President Johnson's Library show confusion and panic among Washington leadership. Calls between the Joint Chiefs of Staff, the National Military Command Center, Headquarters of Commander in Chief-Pacific and the Secretary of Defense Robert

McNamara were frequently exchanged during the phantom battle. (Vietnam time was 12 hours ahead of Washington time).

Meanwhile, in Hawaii the Pacific Fleet Commander-in-Chief, Admiral Grant Sharp, was receiving flash message reports from the Maddox Captain; these were not voice reports. At 0248 hours in the Gulf of Tonkin, Captain Herrick seemed to do a peculiar thing; sending an additional message where he changes his previous story. Here's where things get confusing.

In Captain Herrick's additional message, he suddenly seems convinced the original ambush was real. "Have interviewed witnesses who made positive, visual sightings of cockpit lights or similar, passing near the Maddox. Several reported torpedoes were likely vessels themselves. Own ship's screw noises may have accounted for some. At present, cannot estimate number of boats involved. TURNER JOY reports two torpedoes passed near her.

At 1608 hours in Washington, McNamara calls Sharp to discuss the incident and asks, "Was there a possibility there had been no attack"? Sharp admits, "Slight possibility". He recommends standing down any retaliatory order against North Vietnam until "we have a definite indication of what happened". As the minutes ticked by some intelligence reports began to conflict with one another. An interrupted SIGINT message, supposedly from one of the so-called attack vessels, reported: "Two planes shot down in the area of battle. We sacrificed two comrades, but all the rest are okay. The enemy ship could also have been damaged".

At 1723 hours in Washington, Air Force Lt.-General David Burchinal, the director of Joint Staff, had been observing the events unfold, from the National Military Command Center. He then received a call from Admiral Sharp in Hawaii. He claimed the new SIGINT intercepted message "pins it down better than anything so far". McNamara felt the report, in addition to Admiral Sharp's belief that the attack was authentic was conclusive enough proof. At 2336 hours President Johnson appeared on national T.V. and announced his intent to retaliate against North Vietnamese targets. It would certainly make for an interesting read to study all Wall Street transactions of the orders placed in defense related holdings, during the hours leading up to this historic proclamation.

Meanwhile, back onboard the Ticonderoga the F-8 pilot and Commander James Stockdale was being ordered to be prepared for a major air strike against North Vietnam, for their "attacks" of the previous evening. Unlike the Maddox's Captain Herrick, Stockdale had no doubt about what had happened: "We were about to launch a war under false pretense, in the face of the on-scene military commander's advice to the contrary".

On August 7th, 1964 Congress approved the "Gulf of Tonkin Resolution". Three days following, Johnson signed it into law. No approval or oversight was required by Congress. Historians' suspicions have always voiced doubts that the second attack in the Gulf of Tonkin ever existed. They also believed that the resolution was based on very flimsy evidence, especially when it came to declaring war. More than forty years later, over 200 documents have been released, along with tapes. They have finally revealed what those historians could never prove.

It has been revealed that "there was no second attack". In addition, the findings reveal a deliberate and disturbing attempt by Secretary of Defense McNamara to distort the evidence and mislead the Congress. One of the most revealing pieces of evidence is a study of the Gulf of Tonkin Incident by NSA historian Robert Hanyok. It has been published in the classified "Cryptological Quarterly". Hanyok performed a comprehensive analysis of SIGINT records from the nights of the attacks. He concluded there was indeed an attack on August 2nd, but the attack on the 4th (the one responsible for both the resolution and the Vietnam War) did not occur, despite claims to the contrary by President Johnson and Secretary McNamara.

A near 90% of the SIGNT intercepts that would have provided conflicting accounts of no 2nd attacks occurring, were kept out of the reports and sent to the Pentagon and the White House. Hanyok also uncovered numerous examples of the falsifying and tampering of submitted evidence supporting a second attack had occurred.

With Kennedy removed and the combined, extreme cowardice and apathy of the American people and Washington, America blindly succumbed in surrender to its new rulers of perpetual war, global conquests, destabilization and the destruction of all things they once held dear. With the Industrial Military Complex unleashed it plunged into an orgy of vile, illicit and corporate greed as a vulgar and immoral pandemic. It spread unabated throughout Southeast Asia as "The Berserker" (Google this painting of Frank Frazetta's), lusting in its compounding, dirty wealth, dousing noxious, residual and toxic chemicals from overhead in a total disregard for women, children and even its own men. And yet to this day, it still lusts for more.

If you are a sovereign nation truly not ever wishing this menace to ever enter your solemn civilization, then that moment in time has arrived for you. By pulling the sword from the stone which Americans, cowering in fear, have failed to do, you would be wise to sever all ties with this beast.

Of all the travesties in American history ever committed by its Zionist crime cabal, "The USS Liberty Incident" ranks at the top of the list. Created by its very own Queen to their new colony Israel, her actions were most outlandish and unprecedented, yet still a perfect match for "The Lavon Affair" stencil. Time after time the world grows ever more weary, sick and tired in Israel's display of its psychotic, abnormal, demented and deranged hate for Muslims; always concocting new false-flag schemes, portraying Muslims as the fall guy for their grotesque misdeeds.

In 1967 Israel attacked the USS Liberty using "unmarked" French built, high performance Mirage jet fighters. The crafts were equipped with both cannon and rocket fire. They succeeded in killing 34 American U.S. servicemen onboard with cannon aircraft, rockets and napalm. While the heat of the battle was in full engagement, it quickly turned to execution as Washington repeatedly ordered the Liberty to "stand down" and not return fire.

Retired Admiral Thomas Moorer, former Joint Chiefs of Staff Chairman stated, "It was one of the classic all-American cover-ups". The Admiral spent a year investigating the attack and was part of an independent panel formed by himself and other U.S. military officials. Former U.S. ambassador to Saudi Arabia, James Atkins was also a panel member.

A former attorney for the Navy who aided in leading the military investigation said that President Johnson and his Secretary of Defense Robert McNamara ordered that the inquiry conclude the incident was an accident. Retired Captain Ward Boston in a signed affidavit released at a Capitol Hill news conference, announced that Johnson and McNamara told Navy officials heading the inquiry to "conclude that the attack was a case of mistaken identity, despite overwhelming evidence to the contrary".

Moorer asked from his wheelchair at the news conference, "Why would our government put Israel's interests ahead of our own"? Moorer, who has long held that the attack was deliberate, wants Congress to investigate this horrid travesty. Israel had claimed it had mistaken the Liberty for an out-of-service, Egyptian horse carrier the El Quseir. According to a 1981 NSA report on the incident the El Quseir "was approximately one-quarter of the USS Liberty's tonnage, about half its length and offered a radically different silhouette".

What clearly comes to light is new suppressed findings. Israel not only purposely attacked this U.S. vessel but it strategically chose to use "unmarked aircraft" to appear as "Arab Republic fighters". An Israeli pilot approached Liberty survivors some 15 years after the attack holding extensive interviews with former Congressman Paul McCloskey, about his role.

According to this senior Israeli lead pilot he recognized the USS Liberty vessel immediately to be American. He relayed this to his headquarters and was told to ignore the American flag and to continue his attack. He refused to do so, returning to his base where he was swiftly arrested and jailed. A dual-citizen Israeli Major later told USS Liberty survivors that he was in an Israeli war room where he listened to that pilots radio transmissions. The attacking pilots and everyone in the war room were all well aware they were attacking an American ship, the Major said. He later recanted the statement after he had received death threats via phone, from Israel.

The Israeli pilot's protests were also picked up by U.S. Embassy monitors in Lebanon. This radio monitor evidence was confirmed by then U.S. Ambassador to Lebanon, Dwight Porter. Syndicated columnists Robert Novak and Roland Evans interviewed Porter who offered to submit to furthering questioning by authorities. Evidently, no one in the U.S. yellow-bellied government had any interest in listening to first-person accounts of Israel's butchery.

Finally, insider sources have confirmed that it was an "unsuccessful false-flag" (FF) operation. Using unmarked aircraft, higher ups in the Israeli war room had intended to purposely sink the ship and blame it on Egypt. The former Joint Chiefs of Staff Chairman, Admiral Thomas Moorer, who was a top legal counsel to the official investigation, was in a position to know. The Admiral agrees that Israel purposely intended to sink the USS Liberty, blame Egypt for it and thereby drag the United States into a war on Israel's behalf.

These highly illegal tactics have shown it to be a continuing pattern of the highest crimes committed by Israel, all dating back from "The Lavon Affair" to "The 9-11 Incident" to "The ISIS Formula", etc., etc., with too many to list in between.

The duality of American perception resorts to seeing what it wants to see. Non-reality, or dream-reality and unipolarity are one in the same thing. The West's sheeples might find an effortless security in the instant gratification of thumb-sucking, clinging to their blankies and bowing into their self-hypnotic state of digital pocket screens, submerged securely in the self-indulgent clouds atop their minds. As the herds all chant in unison, "Yes, yes, I can believe that, oh I would not question that", all that remains within this empire's slide is a fattening before the slaughter. It's heavily guarded airport floors will someday be littered knee-deep in one-way ticket stubs, of those who've escaped to a multipolar world.

History, like people chooses to remember what it wants and forgets what it wants. One thing which it has taught is that humankind can make great nations, but that it takes even greater people to keep them that way. Far from the political thunder of Western election campaigns where bullhorn proclamations and soapbox promises each echo their solemn declarations of getting tough with Wall Street, stands the memory of one great man who history seems to have chosen to forget. That man was Ferdinand Pecora.

Born in Nicosia, Sicily in 1882, he and his parents immigrated to the United States in 1886. On the west side of Manhattan, New York in New York City he grew up in the section of Chelsea. After a brief stint studying for the Episcopal ministry he was forced to leave school when only a teenager, due to his father's injury in an industrial accident. Pecora was fortunate enough to land a job with a Wall Street law firm as a clerk. Eventually he attended New York Law School and in 1911 he became a member of the New York bar. Pecora's political affiliations were originally Progressive Republican, yet later he joined the Democratic Party and became a Tammy Hall member in 1916. At the age of 36 he was appointed an Assistant District Attorney in New York City.

Over the decade which followed, Pecora became increasingly well known as a bright and just prosecutor. Though he had limited experience on Wall Street, Pecora helped close more than 100 businesses of illicit activities, also known as "bucket shops". He was appointed Chief Assistant District Attorney in 1922, placing him as the number two man under newly elected Jacob Baton. Seven years later Baton chose Pecora as his heir apparent, but fearing that the honest Pecora might possibly begin prosecuting some of its own members, Tammy Hall declined to nominate him.

Pecora began his own private law practice, having left the District Attorney's office and was content enough to remain there until 1933. In a quantum leap, Ferdinand Pecora was suddenly appointed Chief Counsel to the United States Senate's Committee on Banking and Currency. This was during the last months of the

Herbert Hoover presidency and his appointment was made by an outgoing Republican Chairman, Peter Norbeck. Pecora then continued his appointment under a Democratic Chairman, Duncan Fletcher. This moment in history was at the bottom of The Great Depression, just following the 1932 elections which brought Franklin D. Roosevelt into the White House and saw the Democratic Party in control of the Senate.

The Senate hearings which Percora led investigated the causes of the 1929 stock market crash and major reforms to the American financial system were launched. Pecora was joined by John Flynn, a journalist and Max Lowenthal, a lawyer. Together they personally spearheaded many of the interrogations at the hearings. This line-up of characters included some pretty heady Wall Street personalities such as Richard Whitney, then president of the New York Stock Exchange, George Whitney, a partner in J.P. Morgan and investment bankers Thomas Lamont, Otto Khan, Albert Wiggin of Chase National Bank and Charles Mitchell of National City Bank (now Citibank). Due to Pecora's work and his being well known as honest, the hearings quickly adopted the popular name, "The Pecora Commission". Time magazine even featured Pecora on the cover of its June 12th issue in 1933.

Pecora's investigations uncovered illegal practices in the financial markets which benefitted the 1% at the expense of ordinary investors. Among them were the exposure of J.P. Morgan's "preferred list", showing the bankers influential friends such as Calvin Coolidge, the former U.S. president, Owen Roberts a Justice of the U.S. Supreme Court who participated in stock offerings at steeply discounted rates. Pecora also revealed where National City (Citibank) sold off bad loans to unsuspecting Latin American countries by packaging them into their financial products. He exposed investment banker Albert Wiggins of Chase as having shorted Chase shares during the crash. Pecora uncovered Charles Mitchell of National City (Citibank) and top officers who received $2.4 million in interest-free loans from the bank's coffers.

Encouraged by these findings, the United States Congress enacted the Glass-Stegall Act (later removed by President Clinton), the Securities Act of 1933 and the Securities Exchange Act of 1934. In the deep throws of The Great Depression, Pecora's proceedings depicted the class extremes between an elite group of white collar criminal affluence and the majority of Americans living in absolute poverty. Under Percora's questioning J.P. Morgan Jr. and many of his partners admitted they had paid no income taxes for the past two years.

Upon closing his investigations President Roosevelt appointed Ferdinand Percora a Commissioner of the Securities and Exchange Commission. Pecora wrote a book of his Senate investigations in 1939 titled, "Wall Street Under Oath: The Story of Our Modern Money Changers". In his memoir he states, "Legal chicanery and pitch darkness were the banker's stoutest allies".

The only difference between Pecora's era and today is that the names have changed, but the banking entities are still the same ones. Any and all laws to safeguard ethical practices have since been removed, or loop-holed to death. You see God forbid, but if Ferdinand Pecora had been shot back then it would have guaranteed that an endless wave of angry mobs, all fighting to personally choke and hang the "banksters". So his good deeds were not in vain.

Kennedy on the other hand, also worked diligently to improve people's lives and safeguard the country. In fact, he was the only sitting American President in history to ever refuse his annual salary! Yet when he was cut down in cold blood for all the world to see the only thing remaining was a Pax Americana who coldly, cowardly, maliciously and degenerately proved, that all this man's hard earned efforts in courage for his people were in vain. His "We the people" completely dropped the ball, never again to pick it up. They surrendered as if upon reflex and immediately cast all this brave leader's achievements to the wind. His fate was no different than a heroic soldier's completely unappreciated valor!

Following the time period after the Project for a New American Century (PNAC of Kristol & Kagan) constructed its policy objectives, one stood out over all the rest and that was to create "a Pearl Harbor type event". Members of a covert, felonious subsidiary of Washington's Zionist cabal, mixed with certain and questionable members of the Mossad, CIA, banking and finance, media, Pentagon and specialized contractors, who frequently met in the deepest of secrecy. They sought to devise an occult plan which would greatly reward every spectrum of their lustful ideologies, while immensely filling the coffers to their insatiable appetite for super wealth.

Many drafts were proposed until they finally achieved a strategic grid that was a feat of masterminding genius. This would later be known as "the crime of all crimes" taking on a life all its own and seemingly created by the devil himself. Its requirements entailed enormous funding and ultra-precision, super-sensitive planning, timing and synchronization. Hijacking the steering wheel of a superpower proved to be a daunting task.

It has been proven that from the time of the Johnson administration to the present day, during these 50 years some $8 trillion have come up in the Pentagon budget as being "unaccounted" for. It is believed that as much as $2 trillion of that revenue went into funding "The 9-11 Event", from the time of its inception to the end of the Iraq war. The 9-11 grid called for highly sophisticated, remote control transponders capable of steering commercial airliners with pseudo-hijackers onboard.

Early morning, pre-chosen airliner craft would be sequestered and crashed into skyscraper targets. Media intelligence suggested commencing the events during early morning to capture a majority of Americans still in a sleepy stupor. The psychological impact would then render the longest effects, lasting at least 36 to 48

132

hours. The first day of the mission required massive disinformation programming relaying to stunned citizens, who conspired the appalling atrocities. In the continuing days media networks would reveal to Americans the identifications and descriptions of those responsible, preferably "religious extremists" or "Muslims". Within 6 to 7 days following the masses were to be force-fed every detail about 19 Muslims hijacking four planes and killing 3,000 Americans.

The symbolic "Twin Towers" of the World Trade Center was picked as the star of this morbid show mainly because it housed more records that insiders and elites wished destroyed, more than any other target. As an encore to symbolize aggression against the military, a contingent charade was also to be enacted at the Pentagon building. Many of the powerbrokers who devised this grand scheme (9-11) still remain in power today. That cast of characters could be found in Congress, the CIA, the Mossad, the Pentagon and Cheney's Bush White House, who all helped assemble the "crime of crimes" like a group of finely tuned surgeons. The number of people in-the-know of the operation were estimated to range from 24 to 50.

There were several Pentagon generals, a small group of U.S. and Israeli intelligence operatives, six or seven White House ideologs and specific, corrupt Congressmen and Cabinet members, some of who were black mailed. In light of their most recent work in sponsoring ISIS and orchestrating many false-flags such as the Mumbai, India Incident, the Boston Marathon Incident, the Malaysian Airliner Incident, the Ukraine Coup Incident, the Syrian Gas Incident, The Paris Incident and The California Incident, it is likely that their future targets will be made more and more domestic.

The only vulnerability to their successes is in any lack of the public sheeples' acceptance of them for face value. But if they didn't seem to care about seeking truth or justice over a president being murdered, then watching another 3,000 Americans leap to their death on their smartphones won't motivate them much either I suppose. This new American and European public of the liberal totalitarian State really appears much more docile than in any other country. Their dispositions are all conditioned towards "crisis initiatives". Translated, this means they refuse to let anything stand between them and their $4 Starbucks frappe, until an armored tank drives up to the café and shoves a loaded barrel through the plate glass window.

"The 9-11 Incident" relied on a cadre of followers, foot soldiers and mercenaries to actually perform the dirty work. A combined team of CIA-Mossad warriors supervised the laborer-technicians who planted the explosives in the weeks and months leading up to the controlled demolitions. Simultaneously, electronic guidance systems were repeatedly tested on airliners. Not much was left to chance.

Somehow top Generals Eberhart, Meyers and Weaver were either over-ruled or corrupted enough to achieve the NORAD system to stand down. Anyone opposing the plan could be killed, contained, or controlled. The planners received phenomenal fortunes, dictator-like powers and a destabilization of the sovereignty. Israel got the destruction of her enemies, while promotions were being churned out over at the Pentagon. Wall Street technocrats were met with billions in profits and the absolute destruction of Security and Exchange Commissions' records, housed in the World Trade Center building.

Intelligence ops and military contractors also found themselves neck-deep in riches and religious autocrats were anointed with a new crusade. It was an orgy of power, profits and pseudo-patriotism. The deaths of a few thousand seemed to them a small price to pay for their ends. The devil never considers his methods to be immoral.

This particular chapter, "The Day America Died; Empires in Decline" covers a very busy period in American history. So busy in fact, that in order to fully comprehend it requires a bullet point review in a bit more textbook fashion. This tumultuous period can be separated into six parts:

1: Presidential Assassination (JFK)

2: U.F.O.'s and Contingencies

3: Earth Damaged

4: Assassination, Tonkin (Vietnam), USS Liberty, 9-11

5: Sanctioning the U.S.

6: The Beast Grows

1: In review: "Presidential Assassination" (JFK):

The anatomy of this act cuts straight to the core of Benjamin Franklin's meaning; "It is not a question of if you will have the government you seek, but how long you will keep it". A nation that kills its leader with permission, sets into motion its demise. America's leadership knew full well the unabated crimes surrounding this tragedy. They permitted themselves silenced and accepted coercion. This is the precise moment in time "America died".

2: In review: "U.F.O. and Contingencies":

Secret societies have no great powers. The only thing outstanding about them is the fact that they are occult. Kennedy himself called them repugnant. Their only strength is a dimension in your mind, where fear and imagination manufacture it. Exposing covertness neutralizes strength and reveals stigmatism. Like Dorothy in The Wizard of Oz when she exposed the wizard for all to see.

It only makes good sense to have a plan "b" and "c". Just remember though, so long as you permit these "Agents of Chaos" as journalist Pepe Escobar calls them, to operate unquestioned they will always carry around several contingency plans up their sleeves. And "attacking you" can always be made one of them.

3: In review: "Earth Damaged":

We are no less ignorant than our Roman forefathers. My personal conclusion to the reason The Roman Empire fell are many. It's failure to cultivate their minds, rotate crops and promote small farming, implement a better system of law and justice, practice discretionary oversight, protest unjust wealth distribution, demand accountability, cut unnecessary waste, spending and debt, seek partnerships over division and to create cohesion over legions were all contributing factors to the Roman Empire's demise.

If you can stop long enough to "be in the present tense" for a moment and take a good look at the world you live in, the Americans, Europeans and all other so-called "fully developed" nations of today, are now no less guilty of these exact same shortcomings. Rome was a unipolar empire just like the West. Unipolar empires always make the same misstep of not seeking to assimilate themselves into their environments. Like an anti-matter they always choose to conquer them, even nature itself and eventually, their own people. The Romans often salted their enemies' field crops; today we have Monsanto invading India with GMO's. Salt, GMO's, not much difference. Unipolar empires never initiate coexistence, they always seek domination, division, destruction and destabilization. To read history is one thing, but to learn from it is quite another.

4: In review: "Assassination, Tonkin (Vietnam), USS Liberty, 9-11":

Replacing the checks and balances of your democracy with hegemonic tyranny means that your nation is already pillaged and if not stopped in its infancy you will find yourself trying to escape it.

5: In review: "<u>Sanctioning U.S.</u>":

The U.S. of today not being the one of its first 187 years, finds itself now serving as an Israeli colony. Both are now "Terrorists States", that meaning they both support state-sponsored terrorism; they condone it, practice it, support it, fund and train it, arm it and then kill just a little bit of it. Both now have a global reputation for insisting to continue the practice of camouflaged "false-flag events" to unjustly frame the Muslim world as their fall guy.

Well you make your bed and then you have to lay in it. The West will wake up too late to the fact that they need those Muslims "economically", twice as much more than they realize. So they better not come crying to me or you the day they wake up to find that the entire Muslim world, along with most of the remaining free world, decided to "sanction the U.S.".

6: In review: "<u>The Beast Grows</u>":

By the shear act of publishing this book I have my head inside the lion's mouth and it is untamed. Though the New World Order's (NWO) unipolar beast sinks slowly in the quicksand of its final throws it has demonstrated without hesitation, its lust to kill includes even its own kind (Americans).

There's a nature video once made of a grizzly bear eating over a handsome catch of freshly caught salmon, who is suddenly visited by a wolverine. After several attempts to try and steal the salmon the wolverine finally surrendered this standoff, but before he left he proceeded to urinated all over the bear's entire catch.

As multipolar nations, former allies and more and more Americans, slowly begin to distance themselves away from this beast (NWO), be always aware of its complete ineptitude to be satisfied and its disposition to destroy all that it cannot have.

Chapter Four

Cross-border Healthcare, Medical Tourism and Healthy Economics

When visiting my father in upstate New York, I came down with a severe 48 hour bug. After blood and urine tests and an x-ray I was given no medication, a bill for $1,700 and I ended up curing myself. "BUYER BEWARE"! The U.S. medical profession has picked up where the investment bankers left off!

Since the 19th century wealthy patients from lesser developed regions of the globe would travel to medical centers in the United States and Europe, for cures and treatments not yet available in their own countries. Then in the early 1990's, that traffic trend began to reverse in the opposite direction.

Today cross-border healthcare patients are fleeing the rapacious and exorbitant "medical profit centers" of the unipolar world to escape from its healthcare highway robberies. Patients in fully developed countries today are just fed up with costs, inaccessibility, undesirable formats, overburdened public health systems and long waiting periods. In the past 10 years the global healthcare market has exploded in Southeast Asia, clocking more than five million new foreign visitors. The cross-border healthcare industry has reached the $40 billion mark, with an annual growth rate of 20%.

Southeast Asian countries such as Singapore, Thailand, India, Malaysia and the Philippines are the new frontlines in overseas appeal, followed by Latin America, the Middle East and Russia. At New Delhi's Apollo hospital in India, regular heart surgery charges average $4,000 compared with a $30,000 average in the United States. A "nose job" in India averages $850 and $4,500 in the U.S. An MRI in Brazil, Costa Rica, India, Mexico, Singapore, or Thailand will run you from $200 to $300. In the U.S. it can be three to four times that.

It is my own observation that not everyone is an overseas candidate for health procedures. Local customs and methods have proven to be too much for some ole-fashioned, die-in-the-wool types seeking heavy strokes to their ego, while preferring to run to a doctor every other week just to get their blood thinners readjusted. But one shouldn't forget the unipolar world does actively "promote hypochondria"! The amount of unnecessary doctor visits in the West annually (which I'll discuss later on) is astounding.

I can recall the first time I stepped foot inside a China medical clinic. It was during a colder time of the year (about 45 degrees), yet every window was flung wide open with the curtains flapping inside at nearly a right angle and all the patients in the waiting room still had their winter coats on. I could nearly see my breath. When I confronted my doctor about it he replied, "Oh hospital windows closed in China not good; keeps the sick inside". Ha, the funny part was I had never stopped to consider that before, but he was probably right. The places people seem to get sick most often are in hospitals and schools. I must add that luckily I had a Chinese girlfriend at the time who always expedited my visits. But anytime I went there they always succeeded in curing me pronto and for 80% less than it would have cost me back in the States. Most all of visits were dysentery related (eating in greasy spoons I should have passed up) and I later survived the notorious SARS outbreak unscathed.

Luckily today the foreign medical services will shock you in how much neater and cleaner they are than here in the West. Quite a few can give you the sensation you're checking into a 5 star hotel. Champion Global Healthcare, a subsidiary of Blue Cross, Blue Shield of South Carolina, includes some 13 hospitals in its network around the world that have been accredited by the Joint Commission International (JCI). JCI is known as the "Good House Keeping Seal of Approval" for foreign hospitals, having accredited more than 170 of them outside the United States.

Let's stop and face some facts here. Doctors in other countries not only live in a lower cost environment, but they get paid far less and their school tuitions are next to nothing in comparison to Western systems. Also too, most of them don't even have a car, but use public transportation and they have not been indoctrinated by their culture that they all deserve to drive Porches, have membership at the finest country clubs, or be able to send all their kids to Ivy League schools. Most foreign doctors graduate with zero student loans! If Americans were seriously interested in drastically reducing the cost of healthcare they can start with "the cost of education". That and getting all corporate pharmaceutical companies the hell out of the medical profession, at least in terms of coercion.

An estimated 6 million American patients-a-year are booking round-trip flights to destinations such as India, Thailand, Singapore, Malaysia, the Philippines, Mexico, Russia, UAE, France and Belgium to secure cross-border health services. Devon Herrick, Senior Fellow with the National Center for Policy Analysis in Dallas commented, "People are going abroad for necessary medical treatments such as knee and hip replacements and cardiac procedures. In many countries, especially places like India, the quality is very high and the price can be up to 80% less expensive".

David Boucher is the founder and president of Champion Global Healthcare. He states, "The cost of healthcare in the United States, combined with the fact that we have a shortage in this country of physicians and probably more acutely, nurses collides with the Silver Tsunami which first hit in 2008 and saw a rapid increase of Americans turning age 62", he noted. "Over half of the folks turning 62 opted for Social Security and most do not have an employ-sponsored medical program. There's going to be a sharply increasing number of people needing bypass surgery and hip and knee replacements".

More post-50 Americans are considering overseas alternatives, also popularly termed "medical tourism". Being once something only enjoyed by the wealthy, medical tourism is "really turning into something people can enjoy" says Josef Woodman, CEO of Patients Beyond Borders which provides guide books on medical travel. "Our population is continuing to age into financially challenging procedures", Woodman commented. "Every month the insurance companies find a way to take benefits off the table. Each month there is a slightly bigger piece of the population pie that is going to find the cost savings very attractive".

Rajesh Rao, CEO of Indus Health mentions, "I would tend to say that 80% or more of the people using medical tourism are baby boomers. I would say the bulk of the utilization happens with baby boomers just because they're at an age where they need more intervention". Mr. Rao's company is a medical travel program provider for patients and employer healthcare plans.

Most people seeking cross-border healthcare for treatments that are unaffordable in the U.S. choose to pay out of pocket. In contrast to what they're saving, those savings can be as great as 80% including airfare! And for those 17% of Americans between the ages of 45 to 64 who were uninsured as of 2010, an extra $25,000 to $35,000 of savings can mean the difference of having to refinance their home and being out of thousands dollars.

So given all of the cost incentives, why hasn't cross-border healthcare taken off? "We're so used to the adage that 'you get what you pay for', it takes a little thinking outside the box" says Rao. "By just going outside you end up getting a lot better quality and a lot better healthcare for a lower cost. Until you actually see it, it's hard to believe". In a 2009 Gallop poll, 29% of Americans responding said they would consider going overseas for "alternative treatments for a major medical problem". However, that number jumped to 42% when asked, if "the treatment were cheaper and the quality similar to that found in the U.S.

The number of International hospitals who've spotted this trend are swiftly jockeying for enhanced certifications, which can enable them the ability to cash in on this growing market. It not only makes for smart business practice, but it gives their new onboard patients a sense of self-assurance. The genie is out of the bottle you might say. It's just another organic reason for escaping to the multipolar world.

The Joint Commission International (JCI) mentioned earlier, has not only placed its seal of approval on 170 foreign hospitals, but an additional 299 other foreign medical organizations. The JCI-accredited Fortis Hospital in Bangalore, India, has exceeded the majority of its foreign patients' expectations and is affiliated with Harvard Medical International.

One patient shared his experience: "They picked me up at the airport at 4:00 AM and took me to the hospital for x-rays. My room was incredible, the care phenomenal. I was there in the hospital for 7 days and I was in what I would consider to be a four or five star health facility. They rolled me into surgery at 8:00 AM and I was under the knife until noon. When they got me up I was pain-free. I could not believe it." This patient was once a professional caddy on the PGA and LPGA tour circuit. But a crippling pain had taken him off the course and into a wheelchair for more than 60 days.

He found himself with excruciating pain, while practically living on Tylenol and Aleve. He couldn't stand up straight and was hunched over. Towards the end he could make it with a cane, maybe a 100 yards and then he was toast. After living with this pain nearly four years his options were limited. He was uninsured and unemployed due to languid disc problems in his spine. Once an orthopedic surgeon offered to treat him free-of-charge, but after further examination he realized the patient's condition was far worse than anticipated. The patient commented, "I exercised every possible avenue I could in terms of getting public assistance to get some medical healthcare, but I kept running into dead ends".

Now here he was in Bangalore, India getting treated like a king and suddenly finding himself completely cured. He was pain-free for the first time in 5 years and all for pennies on the dollar. "The first thing the doctor said after my surgery was, 'My, you're a lot taller than I thought you were"! The patient has since confided "I had nothing negative happen to me, so I would promote it 100%". Now, could you imagine what will happen should the unipolar world's "New World Order" succeed in its quest?

Linda Beier was an expatriate living in Hong Kong. She'd long been unhappy with her teeth's appearance and after learning of a friend's plan to vacation in Thailand for 10 days, she decided to pencil-in a quick appointment to a reputable dental clinic in Bangkok and join her. Her problem was fixed to perfection for substantially less than any services found back in Hong Kong.

Several hospitals in Asia have established some outstanding reputations for themselves on this ever-growing medical tourism circuit. Countries like Singapore and Thailand have set up government agencies to assist in marketing their highly acclaimed healthcare services on a global scale. Medical travel agencies are beginning to crop up all over the planet. Many top Asian hospitals now offer international desks and specifically cater to cross-border patients with everything from scheduling to booking hotels.

U.S. based MedRetreat is an exclusively medical tourism agency. Catering to North Americans, it arranges hospital treatments in 10 destinations, including India, Thailand, Malaysia, Latin America and South Africa. It's equipped with "destinations program managers" trained to join patients in route to all appointments, while the agency coordinates transfers and books your hotel.

It comes as no surprise that Americans are looking elsewhere for medical alternatives. The prestigious Commonwealth Fund put out a 2014 report ranking the U.S. at the bottom of its list of all industrial nations, for accessibility and affordability of healthcare. The U.S. based medical Tourism Association (MTA) partnered with George Washington University to consolidate information on the benefits of cross-border healthcare. The survey found that the average patient seeking foreign healthcare spent between $7,400 to $15,000 per trip, which included all travel, accommodations and hospital expenses. This is in stark contrast to an average hospital stay alone Stateside, with costs upward of $18,000. To date, Mexico and India are some of the leading contenders in capturing the larger segments of the foreign healthcare pie.

Thailand's Bumrungrad International in Bangkok sparkles with some astonishing appeal for any would-be foreign patient, no matter what origin. The hospital began a $100 million expansion in 1997. Boasting 21 stories with a 10th floor Sky Lobby it was pressed to start courting foreigners early on, due to the great repercussions from the 1997 Asian financial crisis. Today more than one million patients-a-year are treated here and of those, more than half a million are international patients from more than 190 countries, according to the hospital's 2013 statistics.

Bumrungrad's procedural selection offers just about anything, from check-ups to intricate surgeries, to cosmetic enhancements. Whether you're American, Australian, Vietnamese, or Arabian patients stroll in from nearly every pole under the sun. In 2014 Bumrungrad Hospital's entire costs for Coronary Artery By-pass was $18,440. The Same Cardiac Graft surgery in the U.S. was $44,800. Surgical bladder procedure in the U.S. runs a patient about $25,000. At this hospital, only $3,000.

A Bunrungrad spokesman will inform you, "We offer a Mercedes product at a Toyota price". At first glance the atmosphere assumes an environment more like a five star hotel than a hospital, plus comfortable lobbies, restaurants, cafés and more. Bumrungrad Hospital is proud of its high quality, international standards, smooth accessibility and fascinating prices.

The hospital focuses on the intentional healthcare tourist, not the accidental ones. Patients feel confident that they won't find themselves severely mugged by American medical shell games of "double charging, multiple compounding, blind-sided technical fees and hidden specialists charges"! Patients can stroll in, have intricate surgeries performed and still leave with money in their wallets. Bumrungrad also offers a "real time" cost averages on their website for actual costs of specific procedures.

The hospital is a one stop health center which offers patient access to more than 1,000 globally trained healthcare specialists under one roof. People arriving for treatments are given the sensation their checking into a five star hotel. Equipped with concierge-style, on tap services and a paperless, electronic medical records system, this total experience is what attracts foreign patients. Many medical tourism packages are being developed and sold by travel agents. The hospital also offers a kiosk inside The Bangkok International Airport.

Bangkok's International Hospital (BIH) is another medical destination, which facilitates the reception and lodging of foreign families and patients. Having treated patients from more than 100 nations, its

International Medical Center caters specifically to cross-border patients. Equipped with a team of multilingual interpreters, it also offers a separate Japanese Medical Center. Another big attraction to BIH is the hospital's network offering 17 locations across Thailand, including some situated within walking distance to the beach.

For some patients, beach rich Phuket offers a different attraction; "sexual reassignment surgery". Phuket also offers full-body CT and 4D ultrasounds. Its subsidiary, Phuket Health and Travel is well stocked with a wide assortment of packages, stemming from plastic surgery and dialysis treatment, to hip and knee replacements and annual check-ups. Another Bangkok favorite is BNH Hospital. Having its beginnings in serving health services such as orthopedic, pediatrics, ophthalmology and dentistry. It is one of Thailand's oldest healthcare centers, seeing some 75,000 patients from over 150 countries annually. The hospital's International Medical Clinic serves cross-border travel service offering immunizations and what the hospital terms "the first comprehensive spine center in Thailand".

Ever wonder how to "live in the present"? To live fully in the present moment, one's awareness must be solely centered on the here-and-now. You are not dwelling on the past and you are not preoccupied about anticipating the future. Theory tells us past and future are illusions which don't exist. From this degree of perception the adage, "tomorrow never comes" would be fitting. Tomorrow as a concept, is stationed in anticipation of what's to come around the corner. If there are shadows around the corner void of any light, is it because "time is now"?

Buddha once said, "The secret of health for both body and mind is not to mourn for the past, or worry about the future, but to live in the 'present' moment wisely and earnestly". Before any of you who are Muslim, Christian, Hindu, Atheist, non-denominational, or otherwise venture any further here, I myself have been a "casual South China Buddhist (ex-Roman Catholic) for 15 years. And as I wrote this Buddha quote, there were two 50 year old statues of the fellow sitting high overhead, on a shelf in a rented studio.

Yet even I must concur that I cannot not often afford to live according to that quote, in a continuing sense. It would almost require one have a constant maid always following you around, just to get you through the day. I am not going to wait until I'm out of sugar to say, "Oh look, I am out of sugar. I will go to the store to get some now", at five in the morning! It would be very interesting to hear a Muslim's, or Hindu's interpretation of "living in the present", as well as all remaining religious sects' perspective.

People who are "present living fanatics" claim we are living in an illusion, if not in the present tense. I have a job here and it is to relay to you "objectively" the interpretations of a rich cross-cut of research. But being myself I would say that any human who's machinery (body and mind) is running smooth and well-balanced is capable of "shifting time" at whatever variable speed they need. Want to be in the past for a moment? Fine, go there! Need to be here now for a moment? Great, do it! Got to think about tomorrow for a minute? It's o.k.!

It is a healthy thing to afford living present tense, but I admire a person who is a "seasoned driver" and handler of time. People who are the most caught up and tangled in "worry" could use a strong dose of "being in the present" break. Yoga theorists too, will argue that people often beat up on themselves for past mistakes and that they need more "nowness". As an initial therapy for relief I agree, but I would insist that people who are out of control mentally, or emotionally have some serious self-confidence issues.

People who find themselves juggling many responsibilities on a daily basis, week in and week out, would benefit most from this type of closure. A time-out, a breather, a break from the grind is vital to replenishing what energies you just sacrificed for some rapacious, inconsiderate company perhaps. Present tense theorists say that if you're living in the present, you are living in acceptance. You're accepting life as it is now and not how you wish it would have been.

For myself "a realist", I see the past as a bit of a "keeper of records" anthology. The future as "an estimate" and the present as "live"! I also "do not always accept" things in the present tense. If a man suddenly burst through the door with a gun, how can I accept that? I could say, "I knew I should have gone out of town this weekend" under my breath, before I react to deal with the present tense.

The "present tensers" go on to believe that when you're living in acceptance you realize everything is complete as it is. Again, I must hint with objection. To be in the present is to be focused or "just being", but to "accept" the status quo is to stifle innovative thought. I think meditation is fine and that everyone needs a system shutdown and ample time to be reflective like quality beach time, or maybe on a hunting or fishing excursion. But I am a bit wary of some of the latest "cosmic trendies" I am trying to interpret here for you. "Acceptance" I feel is a bad prescription. It demonstrates "surrender" and even "obedience" which can make one's mind susceptible to mind-control, if in the wrong company.

To "be here now" can also mean "to be observant". You can observe and watch and see in the present tense without accepting everything you see and that's where the theorists and I split paths. Buddha also had another interesting adage which was, "Everything happens for a reason" and also, my own adage "I am here through a series of mistakes".

I suggest approaching the present tense movement by being eclectic to it and borrow just what elements from it are most beneficial to you. And they do have some valuable things we can all utilize. For instance, they do have it quite right that to live too much in the past or the future dilutes your "personal power". If one chooses to change one's life, it must be done from the present tense. Hence, "Today is the first day of the rest of your life".

Many people may give you their impressions or suggestions on the difficulties and obstacles to achieving a more "present tense existence". Many might say it relates to our living in abstraction, or in a world of symbolism. Others may argue it is due to our awareness of the passing of time, or time as an illusion, which can possibly cause anxiety by one's looking at the past to predict the future. A rule of many present tensers is that a main obstacle to our living in the present, is the fact that we don't "shut-up"; that is to say, constantly talking whether it's to yourself, or others. This eventually leads to one never being in a relationship with reality.

Stories are a good thing in their own time and place, whether you're creating them, or listening to others tell their tales. But to be conceptual is not real, so one should always be aware that we live to a great degree, in a world of symbolism. I will be sharing with you various different present tensers' ways to start living in the present. Living in the present does not mean having to give up stuff. Trading extremes doesn't work here. The object to obtaining being in the present-tense is "balance". Here is one list of 5 ways to possibly achieve that for yourself:

1: "Don't try and quiet your mind". Don't attempt to judge your thoughts. Witness them as if they were sound.

2: "You aren't your thoughts". Think of yourself as a force which moves through your body, mind and spirit.

3: "Be alive with breath". When focusing on your breath you might notice that "it just is". You do breathing and breathing does you. Hence, you have attained the quality of reality.

4: Meditation with music". Pick your cultural favorites, but ones with no words. Some prefer Japanese, Hindi, Chinese, or Middle Eastern; so long as it's instrumental. Some might prefer the sounds of ocean surfs coming into shore (seagulls' o.k.).

5: "Mindfulness". Practicing mindfulness is to remain aware of all our actions. To perform simply tasks at face value is being enough aware not to think of the past and of the future tense. We're "live" and in the moment.

Getting back to "medical tourism", Singapore is one more favorite destination offering safety and convenience with upscale facilities and state of the art technology. Critics review the costs here to be anywhere between 30% to 50% more than Thailand, but still a substantial savings for the value over U.S. facilities. English is the language most widely used here. Singapore set its sights high from the beginning as an international medical hub, not just for medical tourists, but for research conventions and education in 2003. Singapore now ranks as #1 in Asia by the World Health Organization (WHO) and #6 globally.

By simply contacting the Singapore Tourism's Medical Travel Team, medical tourists can start making their necessary arrangements for their trip. Singapore's Tourism Board states that it received some 850,000 cross-border patients for 2012. From transplants to health spas, Singapore boasts the full spectrum in healthcare services. It also has 25% of all JCI-accredited facilities in Asia. Being a popular medical tourist location for many reasons, Singapore is equipped with tourist, leisure, or business packages, as well as emergency evacuation patients coming from man-made, or natural disasters.

eMenders, a group of more than 50 specialists, is based at Mt. Elizabeth Medical Center in Singapore and oversees more than 25 different specialty areas. All of its doctors possess internationally acclaimed qualifications and have received their training at top institutions. eMenders claims it is important to separate the titles "medical travel" from "medical tourists". eMenders' patients are predominantly travelling to Singapore for intended medical services, while there are those who utilize their services to coincide with their trip and/or as add-ons for cosmetic, dermatology, dental and general preventative procedures.

Most of eMenders patients are expatriates from Indonesia, Malaysia, Myanmar, Pakistan and Bangladesh. Procedures most popular with this group are cardiology, urology, gastroenterology, dermatology, orthopedic surgery and neurosurgery. Some patients also seek to compare against a diagnosis made by their doctors back home, as well as to get second opinions on treatments.

Mount Elizabeth Hospital owned by Parkway Group, also owns Parkway East and Gleneagles Hospital of Singapore, in addition to a network of hospitals in Malaysia, India and Brunei. Patients from as far away as the U.K., U.S., India, China and Vietnam come to Parkway's Central International Patient Assistant Center for help in accessing guidance to the correct channel of expertise for medical issues, travel and lodging.

The Specialists Dental Group also attracts cross-border clientele to Singapore. Formerly known as Henry Lee Dental Surgery, its been providing dental care at Mount Elizabeth Medical Center for more than 30 Years. It is now run by Dr. Henry Lee's daughter, Helen Lee and has grown to four locations, with a team of 11 specialists. Cross-border patients here come from Indonesia, Malaysia and Hong Kong and as far away as Australia and New Zealand. Its roster also includes an increasing number of patients from Russia,Canada, the U.S. and U.K. The most popular procedure among them are for dental implants, crowns, veneers and dentures.

Raffles Medical Group is Singapore's largest private practice, with its star Raffles Hospital offering a medical tourist portal in 11 different languages such as Arabic, Bahasa, Russian and Japanese. The hospital sports a wide selection of "fixed-price" packages. Among its most popular specialties are osteoporosis screening and treatments, total knee replacements and coronary artery by-pass grafts, where the latter will run about 18,000 Singapore dollars for as many as 8 nights stay, with two in ICU, plus all expenses included.

Now..., care to venture "back to the present"? Simplification and elimination of clutter and non-essentials can evaporate a chronic bane. When the only moment is the present one for yourself, you might find these interpreted bullet point options helpful in assisting your present-tense attainment. I will of course reserve the right to object:

1: "Remove unnecessary possessions". This can aid a transition to present tense merely because it removes association to past memories or lives. (I would not however, suggest you trash family albums, etc).

2: "Smile"! Though I would suggest it not be a synthetic smile, each day does offer us its own possibilities. Taking ownership with your own attitude, with a sense of "anythings possible" optimism, hones a healthier outlook.

3: "Appreciate the day's moments". Soaking yourself like a teabag in "today's" aromas, sights, sounds, triumphs, misfortunes and emotions. I will have to throw a flag-on-the-play here and suggest you don't include "emotions" and "misfortunes".

4: "Forgive old pains". Harboring resentments can often serve you better if you can convert them into a forgive-and-forget solution. However, this should not be confused with "lowering your guard" against individuals you cannot trust.

5: "Love your job". "Ouch"! Definite flag-on-the-play here. For the most part this aspect can be interpreted positively, but I would not want any of my readers to force themselves to love something they cannot. Five out of seven days-a-week correlates into most people spending 71% of their weekly lives toiling in the likes of working at a job. One can avoid the syndrome of "killing time" from one weekend to the next, in one of two ways. Either find yourself a better job, or try standing back and taking a good look at your current one. You can try focusing on the characteristics of your position that interests you most and also the ones which offer the greater potentials to enhance your career's aspirations, in an ascending direction.

in the future everybody will be world famous for fifteen minutes.

6: "Dream of the future, but work hard today". You can dream large, arrange goals and set plans into motion. Performing work tasks at the higher of your capabilities with a conscientious tone, is the most important process to realizing one's dreams.

7: "Don't ride on past accomplishments". Many of us have had our "Andy Warhol moment", our moment-in-the-sun, our 15 minutes of fame. Do not permit to delude yourself into thinking that any "past", highly acclaimed accomplishments have rubbed any lasting magic off on you. If its "past" it has little to do with what you've accomplished for "today".

8: "Cease to worry". Worry is "a waste" by-product, plain and simple. You can be somewhat concerned, but don't dwell on that concern. It has been proven thousands of times over, that "worry" makes absolutely no improvements to outcome. So it is wisest to rechannel your mental energy elsewhere.

9: "Think beyond old solutions". This measure is genius, since it supports out-of-the-box thinking and nurtures innovative results. In today's world many practices become outdated much more quickly. Don't get your mental wheels stuck in the mud by "well that's the way we've always done it" sort of mindset. Today's solutions demand that "your mind be in-the-loop" with the trending environments, which surrounds the most advanced cultures shared on the planet. Yesterday is gone.

10: Conquer addictions". If you're still trapped in a unipolar locale of the West, caught in the cross-currents of its present evolutionary acceleration, from "the land of opportunity" to "the land to escape", then you're quite familiar with the state of addiction. The Western cultures of industrialized nations are notorious for producing "addictive personalities". This starts at a very early age where its citizenry is constantly conditioned to be both "disposable" and "instantly gratified" in their daily lives.

Addiction is a hostage taker that inhibits (sometimes fatally) your abilities to lead a free life today. Seek help, take active measures and insure the removal of their influence over your life. Setting alcohol, cigarettes and over-eating as working examples, there are verified results of success in conquering these with a person's own method of "self-induced tapering". People who very slowly begin to taper off their intakes to these addictions, until they manage them down to zero, (or in the case of food, to acceptable levels) were more inclined to remain free from the addictions "permanently", than those who opted for more abrupt and drastic deprivations.

Have you ever considered India for your healthcare needs? Perhaps thoughts of tigers, ancient temples and IT boom or call centers might pop into your mind when considering India. You can also add cross-border healthcare to that list. Over the last 10 to 15 years, India has become a growing hot-spot destination for medical tourism patients. In 2014 India saw an estimated 150,000 cross-border patients. Cardiac care is a leading draw for medical tourists to India.

Fortis Escorts Heart Institute is a Delhi, state-of-the-art health institute. Fortis Escorts offers open-heart surgery for as little as $4,500 in contrast to a U.S. estimated price of $60,000 or more. As with most international hospitals in Asia the institute assists foreign patients visas, airport pick-ups, hotels, travel itinerary and logistics.

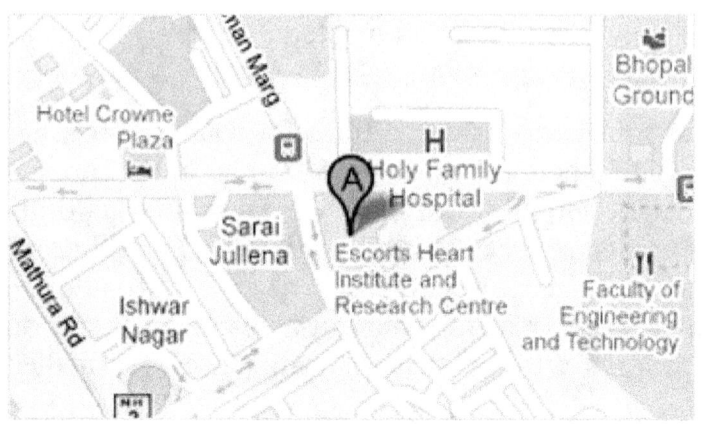

The Indian Department of Tourism states that average healthcare costs in India are about 20% of that of the West. Multi-organ transplants are performed here for about a 1/10th the price in the West. In the U.S. a bone marrow transplant would cost nearly $250,000 or more, but in India the price would equal only about $26,000. And what's more, there is "zero waiting time"! Hip replacements are also popular here. It has been reported that in the U.K., many patients are forced to be put on "waiting lists", waiting many months just to get an opportunity to see a specialist.

    The well known Apollo Hospitals Group has hospital locations throughout India, such as Delhi, Hyderabad, Chennai, Bangalore and Calcutta (Kolkata). It's hospitals in Delhi, Chennai and Hyderabad have been awarded JSI accreditation; cross-border patients are picked-up at the airport upon arrival and swiftly transported to a hospital or a hotel. Another favorite among medical tourists, as well as a large percentage of expats is India's Max Healthcare Group offering 11 locations across northern India, five being in the National Capital region of the Delhi-NCR area. Hospital estimates have tallied one million cross-border patients who are offered an International Services desk and an alignment with health insurance providers from around the world.

Uniquely, many medical tourists are also drawn to India's holistic approach to healing, where the practices of yoga and meditation may sometimes be shared in tandem state-of-the-art techniques. Many city hospitals throughout India offer Ayurveda natural healing centers.

One of these is the outstanding Medanta Hospital, started by one of India's foremost heart surgeons, Dr. Naresh Trehan. Each hospital offers homepathy, natural healing programs and Ayurveda health departments.

The Wockhardt Hospitals Group bears a chain of "superspecialty hospitals" for eyes, bone, joint and heart situations. It has well established locations in Mumbai, Bangalore, Hyderabad, Calcutta and Nagpur. Wockhardt has associations with Partners Medical International and has also developed programs for Harvard Medical School affiliated teaching hospitals.

And in a quick dash to a final four, Jaslok Hospital of Mumbai is highly renowned for its excellent team of doctors for heart procedures. Global Hospitals of Hydcrabad offers a dedicated transpalnt center focusing on liver and heart diseases, haematology and oncology. The Dr. L.V. Prasad Eye Institute in Hyderabad collaborates with the World Health Organization (WHO) for preventing blindness, with locations nationwide.

Lastly, Ruby Hospital of Calcutta has proven extensive services, catering to international patients, with an added enticement. The Ruby is equipped with "The Enclave", its

exclusive "lifestyle" floor which hosts private housing apartments with kitchenettes, computer, 24 hour internet and DVDs. Take in a surgery and grab a holiday in India.

There's still work to be done for attracting medical tourism to the Philippines. One of its most notably facilities is St. Luke's Medical Center in Global City, Taguig, Metro Manila.

Less corruption, drastic reductions in air travel costs, improved airlinks, reduction in airport fees, construction of a transport infrastructure, improved tourist safety, improved security, dealing head-on with quality issues of healthcare, patients' concerns, utilizing better marketing and targeting exact niches it plans to offer, along with the reasons why, make up the long list to its future challenges.

There persists an ongoing stigma about the Philippines and after numerous restarts and failed attempts they've made an unfortunate, global reputation of talking a good story, but inevitably falling short of walking the walk. There remains few excuses why the Philippines isn't an economic powerhouse of Asia. With its rich cultural heritage and a stupendous work ethic, it has always possessed the potential to be a "super-Japan". After years of funding as America's step-child it severed ties like Japan's Okinawa, due to mounting incidents of rape cases involving U.S. G.I.s. Though it still maintains a watered down strategic alliance with the U.S., its biggest roadblocks have always been internally caused by a few bad apples.

The Philippines being as beautiful and as highly talented as it is, I'm confident that they will eventually "set things straight", learn from their mistakes and get it right eventually. It only needs a bit more time, due to its transitional moment in the development process. The Philippines also has a weather system unique to Asia, which in its infancy has been a handicap. Hopefully in the long-term, this will prove to have a strengthening effect in its eventual, determined success.

It's stand alone situation has forced it to be perched fence-sitting with one foot in the multipolar universe and the other in the West. As with Cuba, it stands proud and loyal to its native roots and culture with a very warm and caring peoples. However, if it cannot complete the necessary changes soon it will become forever isolated.

Malaysia is catering well to cross-border healthcare. In the State of Penang, the government actively promotes its private medical facilities for both cosmetic surgery and other procedures. Gleaneagles Medical Center (owned by Parkway Group of Singapore) is equipped with its own medical tourist range of services and packages, such as their standard executive health screening. For just $100 USD it includes eclectrocardiogram, examination, chest x-ray, blood work and other tests.

Penang Adventist Hospital is a 220 bed private hospital, who's network boasts more than 600 centers worldwide. Penang Adventist is the first facility in North Malaysia to offer laser heart surgery and coronary by-pass procedures.

Also in Penang there's Island Hospital, internationally acclaimed, this quite modern facility stands equipped with heart, urology, fertility and laser-vision correction centers. Among its wide spectrum of services, Island has a "premier program" for $150, or a "standard" one for $80. Though many U.S. and other unipolar

citizens are beginning to utilize the advantages of Malaysia's cross-border healthcare networks, its primary patient-clientele comes from Southeast Asia and the Middle East.

South Korea? It isn't the Philippines, but...,. South Koreans have been going under the knife willingly for years. Girls as young as 14 have flocked to get eyelid procedures (blepharoplasty which creates a more Western look) to enhance their beauty. Unfortunately, the nation's plastic surgery sector has suffered greatly, due in part to unqualified doctors posing as cosmetic surgeons, sometimes with assistants performing surgeries and some of which have gone horribly wrong. Be forewarned if you're planning this destination for any cosmetic work.

Vietnam? Though FV Hospital there is highly reputable and offers state-of-the-art healthcare throughout (is in partnership with Singapore's National University Hospital), when considering Asia overall, I personally would pass up the Philippines, South Korea and Vietnam. For a definite sense of assured confidence in Asia, I'd stick with Singapore, India and Thailand!

Does your business or profession have you moving to the Middle East? Dubai's desert Healthcare City could prove to be your paradise of Eden. Its renowned beachfront hotels, outrageous shopping and top-of-the-world towers, makes Dubai Healthcare City in a world class all its own. Founded in 2002, this first

"healthcare free zone" strives to be internationally recognized as the destination of choice for all medical tourists' needs and research. Its pricing comes in as costing about 1/3 more than its Asian counterparts, but that's still 50% less than U.K. and U.S. facilities. The city is also "tax free".

The American Academy of Cosmetic Surgery Hospital (AACSH) offers cosmetic and plastic surgery for patients wanting low-key treatments, mixed with a holiday in the sun. This is all made possible by American's Al Khayal Surgical Clinic. The AACSH

was Dubai's Healthcare City's first hospital, receiving its Joint Commission International (JCI) accreditation in 2009. Patients can select their lodging from penny-pinching apartments to the "6 Star" Burj al Arab. Want to "save face"? Then Singapore, India, Thailand or Dubai may be for you!

BURJ AL ARAB

This is the last of three intermissions covering short presentations on "being in the present", as interpreted from experts on the matter. Life in the present as a 10-step approach, from a variable perspective. First, try replacing sacrificed living for the pursuit of your goals with cultivating mindfulness and being more conscious of life as it happens. Studies show that people are not only more productive when mindful, but seem to even enjoy life more fully. This means enjoying your food, friends, family and almost anything. Perhaps even things we might normally dread such as chores, can seem a bit more of a breeze when presently performed. Some 10 points to finally consider on your way to attaining a mindful living in the present:

1: **<u>Do one thing at a time</u>**: Though this can be true as a Zen proverb like, "When walking, walk. When eating, eat", it will have tendencies to collide with today's workplace. I'm not aware of any Western employers today who don't incorporate "multi-tasking" into their corporate culture. So on this point of the interpreted expert I would have to add, "When it's possible".

2: **<u>Do it slowly and deliberately</u>**: Oh boy. This one is so anti-productive I am going to completely side-step the expert's recommendations (of slowness). Why? Because if everyone practiced it according to the experts' manner we wouldn't have a country. People would be lined up out the door to McDonalds so far, that half the line would miss their lunch or get fired.

Look "deliberately" is fine, but I must disagree here on slowness. I would say "follow through". Make yourself mindful of the execution of your actions and motions by accentuating them a bit more.

3: **<u>Do less</u>**: Well I can see many a corporation won't be utilizing this expert's methods of "present tensing", so flag-on-the-play on this one.

"Speed" has nothing to do with "being mindful", or "attaining a be-here-now" existence. But I would suggest you try and do all things at an "organic pace" such as without too much, if any caffeine, or energy drinks (perhaps tea would be better). Maintain your usual performance, but feel better by fueling your body with healthier intakes.

4: **"Put space between things":** This means, don't overlap your schedules. Amply allotted scheduling affords you to remain organized throughout the day.

5: **"Take 5, do nothing":** You can better treat yourself at this stage by making better use of 10 to 15 minute breaks. During those time periods it's suggested you take in a little silence, become aware of your thoughts, perhaps focusing on your breathing while noticing the world around you (preferably outdoors). Becoming comfortable with stillness can reinforce self.

6: **"Cease worrying":** The past is gone and the future isn't here yet, so why worry about either one? Try remaining just in this one; the present.

7: **"When you're talking to someone, be in the present":** Actually listen to people and avoid being preoccupied in your mind.

8: **"Eat slowly, savor your food"**: Don't cram down food in a rush. Savoring it more actually helps you eat less and improves digestion.

9: **"Savor life"**: Don't desecrate your free time. Tuning into the sights and being mindful of your environment can enable one to elevate the senses to life around you.

10: **"Chores to meditation conversion"**: I would encourage focus. I also have never seen mention of "emotions" in this 10 point list of aids, so I would further suggest to those who allow for frustration to enter their sensory to take 5. You remove yourself from life when you degrade yourself.

Speaking of "removing", how about eliminating unnecessary doctor visits? According to the American Medical Association there are 1 billion doctor visits-a-year in the U.S., 70% of which were deemed unnecessary. With the help of a phone, email, or text all could have been avoided. If you have a doctor who won't refill your usual prescription without a visit to their office then you don't have a doctor, you've a shylock abusing their profession to ream your benefits and pad their bill while causing you wasteful, out-of-pocket expenses for transportation and time lost with your life. So I suggest you both report them and terminate them as your doctor. Then I would advise you to go online and visit: firstopinionapp.com and your problems will be solved, while your benefits will be saved.

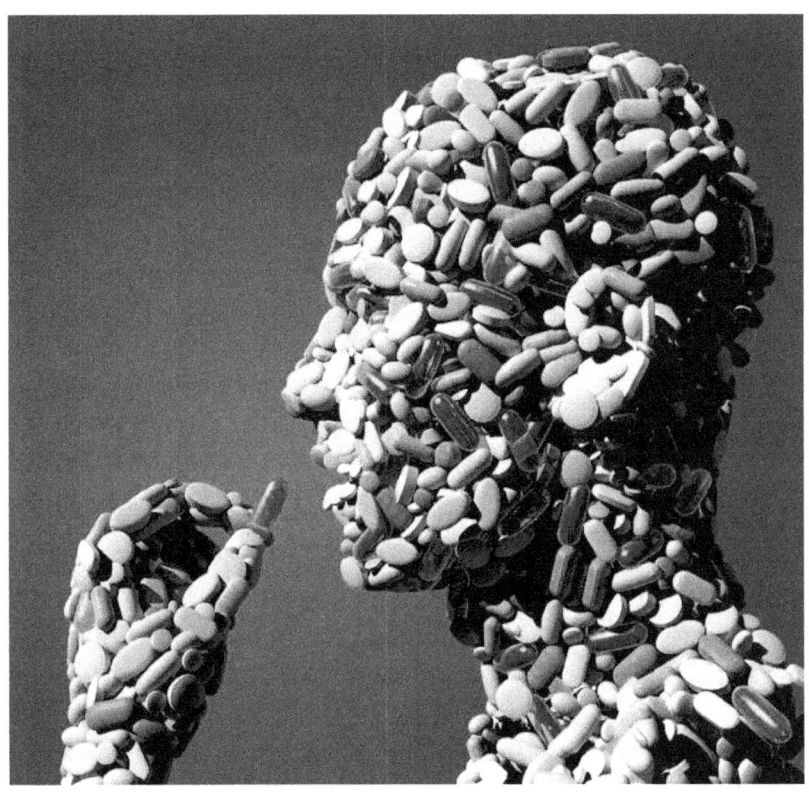

The pill-popping kingdom of the world is the United States where an estimated 13 prescriptions are handed out per every man, woman and child. It has been rated by several poll trackers and individual researchers as the unhappiest nation in the world for 2015. It is also one of the only two nations that permits direct-to-consumer Rx advertising, the third highest medical cost. If you're living in the U.S. you're living in a "pill nation".

During 2013 the average U.S. citizen spent $898 on prescription drugs, a $12 billion industry. Prescription drugs are now the fastest growing sector of U.S. healthcare. The U.S. medical profession is dead, being made evermore in control by pharmaceutical giants who've conditioned doctors to act as dealers. This is no different than the pimps and pushers of the illicit drug trade, out on the streets.

Contrasting in comparison against the U.S. Rx annual costs of $898 per patient are the multipolar nation's $91. Each year Americans spend $4.5 billion on sleeping aids, $7 billion on ADHD drugs and $11 billion on anti-depressants for the unhappiest nation on earth. The time is overdue for a complete retooling of the entire American lifestyle and its society. Obviously a "New World Order" is only working for the rapacious pharmaceutical companies and not the patient. The use of anti-depressants has risen 400% since the 1980's in America where the top 3 money-makers are: #1 anti-psychotic, #2 acid reflux and #3 depression, anxiety and pain.

Today one in two Americans takes prescription drugs, while the vast amount of these witch's potions will not help you and might even harm you. One-in-4 women in the United States takes drugs for a mental health issue. Over the past 10 years the use of anti-depressives among its women has jumped 30%, while the number of overall Americans taking at-least-5-drugs-or-more increased 70%. With anti-depressants comes the risks of the following side-effects: nausea, weight gain, anxiety, headaches, lower sex drive and insomnia.

Between 1995 - 2004 two-thirds of new drugs were "me too" drugs; in essence the same thing, only redesigned. Advertising now constitutes "double" the budgets for research and development in America's drug giants. The evidence is now more than obvious to most outsiders, that Western unipolar concepts of what they consider to be healthcare is actually extremely parasitic and detrimental to good health. So if you're healthy don't visit the U.S. or U.K. A large part in the contributing factor to the West's ills of their people are mostly "lie-related". Many of its citizens complain they are being fed lying propaganda as news, while being forced to accept and believe them it as truth. Add to this the combination of having their "representative" governments no longer representing its voters, but fully representing the graft, corruption, extortion, blackmail and coercion of its corporate-industrial military-Israeli Wall Street powerbrokers.

Time for these people to start utilizing medical tourism, to consider organic medicinals and/or natural cures. Make a profound adjustment to their ways of living. Maybe re-evaluate their circles of friends, get a routine fitness program started, DON'T watch or listen to "main-stream" propaganda houses, but rather replace them with good ones *(I'll post at least 15 alternatives at the end of this book) and yes, don't rule out leaving your country for one that "loves you back"!

The unipolar world they're living in is slowly dying. "Don't die with it"! Take action, push back the madness, adapt to simplicity and "preserve thy self"!

Chapter Five

The Wolves in Sheep's Clothing

What the devil is doing in the details of America is quite simple. First, there was a great "democratic" empire. Then suddenly, only 187 years into it the empire was silently attacked from within by a coup d'e tat systemic virus of deceit and great trickery. The "Home of the brave" then began to turn weak, gullible, sheepish, naive and apprehensive. So they ignored the virus, hoping it would just go away someday.

But secretly and silently the virus proceeded to spread. Devouring, bribing, extorting, blackmailing and threatening any goodness and truth, which ever offered challenge to its wake. The sheepish herds grew ever larger and larger and the devil roared with laughter. "I shall make a profile of you in my own image and likeness. And anyone of you who fits this profile shall be made suspect of all my misdeeds. More and more you will lose privileges, until I finally own your complete body and soul".

The greatest dangers of the West's unipolar world is that it is operated on discontent and periodic destabilization. It creates terrorists, trains them, feeds them, supports, arms them and then

kills them, only not too many. They are the new America's grand fear generator; its top 1%'s excuse to keep dumping more dollars into security and defense, giving them cause to keep pinching back at your rights.

Former Assistant U.S. Treasury Secretary, Paul Craig Roberts once stated, "When the world looks at America, what it sees is an Israeli colony". What Israel and its pals at the Bilderberg Group and in the Industrial Military Complex have done is "manufacture an enemy". More than 95% of the Muslim world lives in peace, promotes and enjoys peace and is peace-loving. Israelis are the opposite. They "love to hate"; to hate and control. So they hate Muslims. And they hate me just as much because I told you.

Their affiliates, Zionist ABC, NBC, CBS and CNN assist them by beating the drums of fear, hype and innuendo as fact, in a black-is-white and white-is-black propaganda. The devil's virus creates false-flag incidents and/or funds actual terrorists to project to the world that all terrorism was created by Muslims. And they keep pounding it into American's heads to "hate those Muslims; we better keep fearing and hating those Muslims", even if we actually "do not"!

And that's what scares the living hell out of this New World Order's demon, is when Americans "befriend Muslims", or "like Russians", or don't believe things as its presstitude press portrays things like The Lavon Affair, The Kennedy Assassination, The USS Liberty Incident, The Gulf of Tonkin Incident, The 9-11 Incident, The Boston Marathon Incident, or the Syria Gas Incident, Paris and California bombings and beyond. So now they've actually started funding terrorists while broadcasting to you "be afraid, be afraid, it's coming to a street near you soon", while profiling Americans who don't believe or support the Zionists news organizations as being "un-American" or "possible dissidents" or "lone wolf suspects".

"When exposing a crime is treated as committing a crime, you are ruled by criminals."

Which brings to mind an old adage my late mother used to tell me when I was a boy, "The devil was sent to hell, because he kept asking questions that he knew all the answers to".

The Bilderberg Group is an annual conference which meets under extra tight security and is not open to the public or press. Usually 120 to 150 individuals from Europe and North America would be brought together with a theme of how to better promote what they've termed to be "Altlanticism". The participants are seen as elite politicians, specialists of industry and also those associated with banking, media ownership and academia.

Its first annual meeting was held at Hotel de Bilderberg in Osterbeek, Netherlands for three days in May, 1954. It was initiated by several people, including a Polish politician in exile, Jozf Retinger. Retinger influenced Prince Bernhard of the Netherlands to promote the concept. The prince heeded Retinger's secret messages and relayed this influential idea to Belgium Prime Minister Paul Van Zeeland and Paul Rijkens, the then head of Unilever. Prince Bernard also contacted Walter Beedell Smith, the then head of the CIA. Smith then asked Eisenhower advisor Charles Jackson to deal with the suggestion.

The first guest list for such a meeting was drafted with 61 delegates in attendance. Its first meeting was deemed a success which led organizers to proclaim an annual conference. A steering committee was established and Retinger was appointed permanent secretary. Conferences were usually held in France, Germany, or Denmark however, there were three held in the U.S., the first American one being held on St. Simons Island in Georgia. All three American conferences (1957, 1959, 1963), were funded by the Ford Foundation.

In 2010 former Cuban president Fidel Castro hinted that Bilderberg lobbyists have full intentions to install a one world government which knows no borders and will have no accountability to anyone, beyond its own self. Over the past 10 years Bilderberg conferences have met in Germany, Canada, Turkey, U.S., Greece, Spain, Switzerland, U.K., Denmark and Austria. Other attendees to these conferences have been David Rockefeller, Henry Kissinger, Bill Clinton, Gordon Brown, Angela Merkel, Alan Greenspan, Ben Bernanke, Larry Summers, Timothy Geithner, Lloyd Blankfein, George Soros, Donald Rumsfeld, Rupert Murdoch, as well as influential parliamentarians, senators, congresspersons and high-ranking CIA and NATO officials.

The Bilderberg Groups' original aim was influencing and imposing Western culture throughout the world, with a tint of morality showing. Daniel Estulin, author of "The True Story of the Bilderberg Group" (2005/2009) states that, "Slowly, one by one, I have penetrated the layers of secrecy surrounding the Bilderberg group, but I could not have done so without the help of "conscientious objectors" from inside, as well as outside the group's membership". Its original intent has been replaced with a pathetic desperation to achieve ultra-wealth and ultra-power in a system no one, but the 1% will like.

Bilderberg elitists now have a new wish list which includes total world domination. They seem posed to attempt this by first "creating terrorists" who will divert attention, while they pillage and crash what remains of the financial system, bubbles bursting in air. Of course a scapegoat will be required for this grandiose fiasco as

Bilderbergers have never been sited taking any blame for their own sins. This is where "the terrorists" come in, but they're in such a panic at this writing they could drastically resort to blaming anyone, Iran, Assad, China, the Russians, or perhaps even "you".

The terrorists serve three purposes. First, for diverting questions away from their financial crimes and secondly, as a grand excuse to continue taking away more of your rights while profiling all as suspects. And third, as a "boogie man" excuse to keep pumped up money for defense rolling in. Just remember the duality at play here. The "NWO gang" created ISIS as a weapon against "you". While their friends in the media pound your head with "be afraid, ISIS is here" programming, it gives the 1% tyrants fast track legislations otherwise deemed illegal. Using terrorism is the smoke of their smoke and mirrors game, creating hastily decided policies under a cloud of war-time-like urgency to get rubber stamped legislation passed. For example, their false-flag Paris massacre is enabling lobbyists to call for U.S.-French NATO Article 5 to be used by putting boots on the ground in Syria. The NWO globalists don't want to eliminate ISIS; they created ISIS to get what they want,

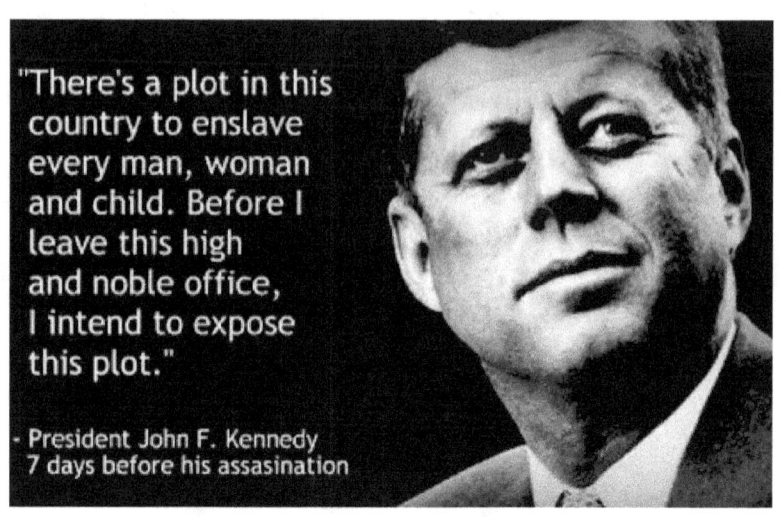

"There's a plot in this country to enslave every man, woman and child. Before I leave this high and noble office, I intend to expose this plot."

- President John F. Kennedy 7 days before his assasination

which was Assad and Syria. This is a challenging moment for the hostage-held citizens of the West.

"ALL WE NEED IS THE RIGHT MAJOR CRISIS, AND THE NATIONS WILL ACCEPT THE NEW WORLD ORDER."

- DAVID ROCKEFELLER

The Bilderberg wish list includes the following:

1: One international identity; one set of universal values.

2: Centralized control of populations.

3: An Order with only rulers and servants.

4: A "zero growth" society, with any increase in power and wealth going to the rulers.

5: Manufactured crisis and perpetual war.

6: Total control of education.

7: Centralized control of all foreign and domestic policies globally.

8: Making the U.N. a world government who'll tax the global population.

9: Expanding secret trade policies.

10: Converting NATO into a global military.

11: Imposing a universal legal system.

12: Creating a global welfare State where obedient slaves are meagerly rewarded and non-conformists are targeted for extermination.

It will be the fall of civilization on Earth as we know it, if with all this power and wealth, the best that we will be able to show for ourselves is an entire planet that's one big, great North Korea.

Here's an update on those rights of Americans, I mentioned earlier. Through enactment of the "U.S.A. Patriot Act" and various executive directives, necessary rights and freedoms once guaranteed to all have now been severely degraded. It is sickening to see the amount of Americans who still do not realize what they have lost:

1: 1st Amendment; "Freedom of Speech". The Patriot Act greatly expands the official definition of "terrorism". Many domestic groups partaking in non-violent protests could soon find themselves "profiled" as terrorists.

The government may now prosecute librarians or "keepers-of-records" if they reveal that the government requested information on their clients. It is now a crime for these individuals (librarians, keepers-of-records) to safeguard your privacy from the government, or tell you that you are under investigation.

194

2: 1ˢᵗ Amendment; "Freedom of Association". Government agencies may now monitor activities of religious and political organizations and then infiltrate these groups with no probable cause, or suspicion of criminality. This is domestic spying on law-biding citizens.

You may now be the subject of a government investigation simply due to the political, activists, or advocacy groups you associate with, or for anything you might have said in their presence.

3: 1ˢᵗ Amendment; "Right to Access Government Information". A U.S. Justice Department directive actively encourages federal, State and local officials to resist and/or limit access to government records through The Freedom of Information Act requests.

The government can now conduct immigration hearings in secret, behind closed doors. These used to be open to the public. Hundreds of thousands of immigrants have already been deported in secret.

4: 4ᵗʰ Amendment; "Freedom from Unreasonable Search and Seizures". Without "probable cause" law enforcement officials may now conduct secret searches and wiretaps in your home or office. They call it "intelligence gathering as a significant purpose". They may also monitor your e-mails, where you go on the internet and record every e-mail and website you've been in contact with.

Law enforcement may now request any records from any source including your doctor, employer, accountant or library. All that's needed is two words, "possible terrorist". Judicial oversight is now handcuffed for searches, when law enforcement uses the terminology "significant purpose" and/or "terrorism".

5: 5th Amendment; "Right to due Process and Freedom from Being Held without Charges". Americans can now be jailed without formal charge and without the right to confront witnesses, or evidence against them. American citizens are now being held in military jails, without charge and without a clear path to appeal for their indefinite confinement. Hundreds of Arab, Muslim and South Asian men were rounded up in Ashcroft raids following 9-11 and held for weeks without charges, until all were cleared of terrorism charges.

6: 6th Amendment; "Right to Legal Representation". Hundreds of U.S. citizens have been detained for months and denied access to an attorney. The government may now monitor conversations between attorneys and clients, in federal jails. The Bush administration filed papers in court arguing an American citizen held in a military jail without charge should be denied access to legal counsel because it would interfere with the process of interrogation.

7: 6th Amendment; "Right to a Speedy and Public Trial". The U.S. Government may now jail its residents and citizens indefinitely, without charge and without a public trial.

8: 8th Amendment; "Freedom from Cruel and Unusual Punishment". The U.S. Government has apprehended and transported individuals they identified as "material witnesses" across the country, holding them for months in solitary confinement, without charge or contact to their families.

The Justice Departments' Inspector General has stated that immigrant men rounded up in the Ashcroft raids following 9-11 (and were later cleared and released), were held in the Metropolitan Detention Center in Brooklyn, New York and were subjected to a pattern of "physical and verbal abuse".

9: 14th Amendment; "Right to Equal Protection". Over 82,000 men of Arab, Muslim and South Asian descent, have been registered with the government under the "Special Registration Program". Over 13,000 are now in deportation proceedings. None have been charged with terrorism.

We have become more aware of the corrupt practices of two sides to the New World Order's triangular cabal; The Federal Reserve and the Israeli-Bilderberg Group, but what of the Industrial Military Complex? Ever wonder what the true cost of the Afghanistan War is? It may surprise you to know, that calculating war costs is a bit like the true-costs rule-of-thumb for automobile ownership. There are various ways to measure war costs. As an example, if you were a war planner for the Pentagon and you found yourself having a want or need for a GM Hummer back in 2009 when the war was fully active, you'd have paid a dealer $35,752 for the little monster. But the vehicle's true cost to own, taking into account depreciation, financing, fuel and insurance, over five years of ownership, comes to $78,616 in "true costs". Paying for war doesn't stop when the battle ends. What's worst, the nation doesn't only pay for its wars over 5 years, but an entire generation. Hmmm, why do I get a faint whiff of global bankers in the vicinity?

It would take "another book entirely" to fully explain the history and relationship between wars and banks. However, I strongly recommend Googling online for an exceptional article, complete with many unique, historic photos', etc., entitled "All Wars, are Bankers' Wars", by Michael Rivero.

The Congressional Research Service (CRS) concluded that the wars in Afghanistan and Iraq has cost taxpayers $1.6 trillion. Alright, but that doesn't give us the true bottom-line. Anyone using that figure to quote a comparison, or otherwise is being more of a GM salesperson than a representative of the taxpayer. By the way did you notice who gets to line their pockets with profits in the war from just this one item you so generously paid for and gave away? The 3 sides of the unipolar triad cabal; one, the Bilderberger's (GM & oil companies). Two, the Federal Reserve (in interest payments) and then three, the Industrial Military Complex's dealers (arms dealers, suppliers) who made the sale.

A more accurate measure of the wars in question comes to between $4 trillion to $6 trillion. Harvard economist Linda Bilmes calculated in 2013, that this accounting includes "long-term medical care and disability compensation for service members, veterans and families, military replenishment and social and economic costs". The folks at the Pentagon don't like talking about war costs, either before or after the crime. A high sticker-price beforehand serves as a cost-effective brake, making their goal (to be at war) a less likely probability. So "war salespersons" (I know it's disgusting isn't it) will always reach for those CRS figures to sell war to the taxpayers, as it muffles opposition.

The Congressional Research Service (CRS) figures had estimated the Iraq War as costing $814.6 billion. The George W. Bush's Administration head of its National Economic Council resigned shortly before the 2003 Iraq invasion, after estimating the war would cost $200 billion. One month later, Defense Secretary Rumsfeld told the public the war's cost would be "something under $50 billion" (didn't this guy used to be a Hummer salesmen?). Linda Bilmes, the Harvard economist stated that the Iraq-Afghanistan conflict alone have been "the most expensive wars in U.S. history". This is before the U.S. entered Iraq "a third time" and before the U.S. decided to keep troops in Afghanistan through 2016.

The ravages of war, something every European, American and unipolar Western citizen must get through their naive, thick skulls soon, are fully funded by them; the wars' blood is on their hands in every taxable transaction of everyday. To fathom wars' true culprits finds us at a pre-dawn moment in unipolar history, which will inevitably burst open its floodgates to a most vile moment. One glimpse of ancient history, to what was once Canaan (Israel) will turn up evidence enough of a similar fingerprint found at the scene of the crime today, within the West's Triad of Death" (Bilderberg-Israel, Bankers and the Industrial Military Complex). There the Israelites eviscerated every man, woman and child into a blood-curdling, historic genocide. If Americans and Europeans don't stop these hooligans dead in their tracks soon, I fear they may all very well find themselves financing their own coming annihilation, by the very same machinery which they funded to protect them!

Rachel Aliene Corrie was born on April 10, 1979. An unarmed peace activist and diarist from the U.S., she was intentionally crushed to death, being slowly run over by an American made, Israeli armored bulldozer in Rafah, the southern part of Gaza. She came to Israel as part of a senior-year college assignment to connect her hometown with Rafah as a "sister cities project".

During her brief stay she became active with other International Solidarity Movement (ISM) members, in the hopes of preventing the Israeli Army's demolition of Palestinian homes. In less than two months after she arrived, following a three-hour stand-off, Rachel Corrie was slowly crushed to death by Israeli soldiers operating bulldozers, who watched her slow execution as it happened. The killing machine was purchased by U.S. taxpayer dollars.

Rachel
CORRIE
The Courage to Resist

On March 16, 2003, Rachel Corrie, a 23-year-old human rights activist, was struck and killed in Gaza by an Israeli military caterpillar while defending the home of a Palestinian family

unitedprogressives.org

Ms. Corrie was raised in Olympia, Washington, U.S.A. and attended Evergreen State College. She was a volunteer in the

Washington State Conservation Corps and was a committed peace activist with "Olympians for Peace and Solidarity". Before leaving for Israel she organized a "pen-pal program" between children in Olympia and Palestine's Rafah child writers.

There are good apples and bad in every race of people. In attempts to bring to light the true demons of war free from prejudice, one may become enlightened to revealing their true identity and intent, in the hopes of daring to interrupt history and prevent more destruction, waste and loss of innocent lives. If one finds themselves in a struggle to fully accepting some variations of Israeli involvement in numerous atrocities such as the Kennedy assassination, The Lavon Affair, The USS Liberty Incident, The 9-11 Incident, The Boston Marathon Incident, The Russian Airliner Incident, the creation of ISIS, the Paris and California Bombing Incidents, then here are some startling and graphic revelations of the actual nature of the beast in question. So graphically repulsive are the descriptions of these firsthand accounts of actual events, that they have been purposely written in as brief and consolidated a format as possible.

More than 200 senior military personnel, intelligence and law enforcement specialists, in addition to two U.S. generals, have concluded having grave reservations with "The 9-11 Incident" and it's commission's report. They have been joined by 1,500 architects and engineers, 250 pilots and flight experts, 400 university professors and 250 survivors. David Griffin, author to 11 books on the subject and a distinguished professor has concluded, "All the proffered evidence that America was attacked by Muslims on 9-11 appears to have been fabricated".

Dr. Alan Sabrosky, former director of the U.A. Army College proceeds with increasing the stakes by unequivocally identifying Israel as the guilty party. Dr. Sabrosky stated, "What we need to stand up and say is, not only did the Israelis attack the USS Liberty, but that it was 100% certain 9-11 was a Mossad operation"!

American taxpayers pay their Israeli master $8.2 million-a-day. A tax imposed on vanquished Americans by their conquerors.

In 2007 President Bush signed a 10 year "Memorandum of Understanding" whereby the United States gave Israel $30 billion for military aid "in a one-lump-sum". In a shape of things to come, allow me to introduce the testimony of Eustace Mullins as he presented the maximum, ultimate extremes of "terror" endured by 66 million Russians, under the crushing ranks of Jewish hegemony.

"There are too many well documented massacres in history, in which the Jews tortured and murdered their victims with the greatest of glee, gloating in such barbaric practices, as tearing out the hearts of women and children and smearing the blood on their faces. The orgy of murder, torture and pillage which followed the Jewish triumph in Russia after the Bolshevik Revolution of 1917, has never been equaled in the history of the world. The Jews were free to indulge their most fervent fantasies of mass murder of helpless victims. Christians were abducted from their slumbers, tortured and put to death. Some were inconceivably sliced into pieces, piece by piece leaving others branded with hot irons and to inflict greater pain by having both eyeballs removed while still alive.

Others were put into boxes with hungry rats gnawing at their bodies, while they dragged others to be nailed to the ceiling by their fingers, or by their feet, then left to die slowly from exhaustion. People were chained to the floor with hot lead poured into their mouths, while others were tied to horses and dragged through the streets to be kicked and stoned to death. Mothers were taken to public squares with their babies snatched from their arms, thrown into the air and caught by bayonets. Pregnant Christian women were chained to trees and their babies cut out of their wombs".

Professor Kevin MacDonald notes bleakly, "We should never forget what happened when Jews were a hostile elite in the USSR. The loathing and contempt for the traditional people and culture of

Russia was a major factor in the avid Jewish participation in the greatest crimes of the 20th century". MacDonald was referring to the systematic murder of more than 66 million Russians under Lenin and Stalin; a period of over 36 years, possessed with mass murders and torture. A Dr. Lasha Darkroom states, "The new American elite is a Jewish elite, exactly like it was in Bolshevik Russia and Stalin's USSR. And it is essentially a hostile elite that loathes the nation it rules".

Professor Kevin MacDonald muses, "It is quite possible that we are entering into a racial dystopia of unimaginable cruelty". James Petras was once quoted as saying, "Over the past 24 months not a single policymaker has voiced any criticism of Israel's most heinous crimes, ranging from the savaging of Gaza to the massacre of the humanitarian flotilla and the expansion of new settlements in Jerusalem and the West Bank. Many of the leading Zionist policymakers rose to power through a deliberate strategy of infiltrating the government to shape policy promoting Israel's interests, over and above that of the United States populace".

Stalin once quipped cynically, "Death solves all problems; no man, no problem". In Otto Fredrich's book, "The Kingdom of Auschwitz", a concentration camp survivor was quoted as saying, "Concentration camp existence taught us that the whole world is really like a concentration camp. The world is ruled by neither justice, nor morality. Crime is not punished, nor virtue rewarded. The world is ruled by power. We are laying the foundation for some new, monstrous civilization".

An innocent victim of that "monstrous civilization" was a Palestinian child who had his arm cut off by an Israeli settler for throwing a stone. Paul Craig Roberts, former Assistant U.S. Treasurer and father of "Reaganomics", once concluded, "America, once a democracy, is now a crypto-fascist country, ruled by a corporate and cosmopolitan elite. There is no freedom, no democracy and no government accountability in Amerika, a fascist state".

Poet-translator Dr. Lasha Darkmoon was quoted, "The Jews fulfilling the wildest dreams conjured up in the Protocols, stand surveying the killing fields of the world they have conquered. Iraq and Afghanistan lie in the ruins, thanks to their machinations. Iran lies in the cross-hairs, awaiting its expected doom. And meanwhile in America, as the body bags are flown in from foreign regions and the lurid circus of bread and games grinds on relentlessly, there is nothing much to live for except sex and death. Stalin's willing executioners, the Jews are now the ruling elite in America. As in Weimar, Germany, the Jews make most of the money and help create a culture of neo-paganism and nihilism, decadence and despair. Nothing has changed except the country. Russia, Germany and America – they all went down like skittles in a row". From George Orwell's book, "1984"; "If you want a picture of the future, imagine a boot stamping on a human face – forever".

After kicking the can down the road for 15 years, the "war on terror" seems more a baton being passed to another generation. It never really was about security of the homeland. The war on terror was a premeditated plan (or mass murder) to disrupt and destabilize Middle Eastern and North African oil economies. Its agenda was about furthering Israel's interests and lining the pockets of commodities dealers, arms dealers, military contractors, the desecration of the Muslim's profile, the burgeoning global heroine supply and the chess-boarding of mercenaries like ISIS to sub-contract the Zionist's dirty deeds. In short, "A New World Order Profit Machine" fueled by perpetual war and highway robbery. Dylan Charles of "The Waking Times" was once quoted, "The war on terror doesn't stop terror, because it is terror".

The world's number one arms exporter per capita is France. The unipolar world consists of arms-for-oil. Destabilization, hi-jacked oil (and/or stolen gold as was Libya's case under Hillary Clinton), then repeat this in the next location. Sounds like terrorism to me. Stefan Molyneux: "You cannot have freedom or peace in a country whose government is engaged in the global wholesale of advanced arms and weaponry to national governments".

So the CIA created the Mujahedeen, which became Al Qaeda, which became ISIS, who is supported by 40 nations including France, the U.K., the U.S.A. and Israel. Again, the wisdom of Stefan Molyneux: "They tax you in order to create weapons to sell to foreigners to attack you". For the first time in U.S. history suicide is, at this writing, the leading cause of death among U.S. soldiers. "Waking Times" editor Dylan Charles (also a student-teacher of Shaolin Kung Fu, Tai Chi and proprietor of "Offgrid Outpost") had this to say: "The goal of the war on terror is to transform the people into willing participants of chaos, mayhem and murder, or to turn them into collateral damage. Nobody is born a terrorist and we are all being set-up as dispensable pawns in an orchestrated clash of civilizations".

David Rockefeller, at a 1991 Bilderberg meeting: "We are grateful to The Washington Post, The New York Times, Time Magazine and other great publications whose directors have attended our meetings and respected their promise of discretion for almost forty years. It would have been impossible for us to develop our plan for the world, if we had been subject to the bright lights of publicity during those years".

The West's unipolar, totalitarian, one world government and population reduction agenda is suffering major defeats. These defeats are not from violent revolutions, great public protests, or citizens pleading with their corrupt politicians. The defeats are related to a wider and wider awakening and a significant portion of the masses frankly refusing to take any actions which offend their conscience.

The Bilderberg-Israeli, Globalist Banking and Industrial Military Complex, power and wealth machine only has two primary tools, which are well known to anyone who reads alternative media: secrecy and deception. Their criminal enterprise will end as millions more, if not billions keep awakening. Since the 1990's researcher David Icke has believed there would be a point in time when this Triad Crime Cabal and its New World Order agenda finds itself suffering from over-exposure. Fortunately that is the moment the agenda is most vulnerable, which explains its desperation in frantically blowing up the Russian airliner and creating the Paris-Brussels attacks.

They're at a point in time where their false-flag operations are becoming sloppier and more hastily planned, as if concocted on-the-fly with less preparation and thought. Just take in a small sliver of their news networks and all you can hear is "be afraid, be afraid, hate Muslims and surrender more freedoms for your own safety"! Doesn't sound like a very confident bunch of ideologues to me. Not when they're having to bait-and-switch by resorting back to their old standard, Israeli textbook stenciled format of "killing the people themselves" to entrap others.

Ron Paul is another litmus test that shows the Bilderberg-Israeli, Globalist Banking an Industrial Military Complex Crime Cabal is failing terribly. He received more campaign donations from U.S. military G.I.'s than any other candidate. This exposed the fact that there's a continuing erosion within the Industrial Military Complex's own foundation and a growing tide of disapproval from within the military itself. Consumer money flows are continuing to migrate increasingly into Credit Unions to escape corrupt banks. Meanwhile, the "fake" war on drugs deep, dark secrets continue to surface. In the U.S. it is now common knowledge that the drug war is a fraud. Small time street dealers are arrested and put into cages, smaller than the ones at their local city zoo. Simultaneously, the U.S. government intelligence personnel imports large quantities of cocaine and heroin to help fund their war operations. U.S. troops now openly admit they're in Afghanistan to support the heroin trade.

From 2004 to 2010 the average net worth of a member of congress rose 15%. For the average U.S. citizen it dropped 8%, while currently the U.S. government's approval rating is heading for single digits. More parents are questioning their children's vaccines, many now going overseas to multipolar world doctors. People are also pushing back multinational commodities giants, such as Monsanto.

And so the exposure and signs of the New World Order being now on the wane continues to gain evermore traction. One might further help things along by boycotting all corporate sponsors of the Bilderberg Group itself. In the words of one late, great musician who professed to have once kissed the sky, "When the power of love overcomes the love of power, the world will know peace", Jimi Hendrix.

We find ourselves living in a 21st century society of feudalism, with most of us serving as the serfs. Many in the West sense an ever tugging undertow into a lower standard of living. Upon first glance you might say that defeating the Triad Crime Cabal's New World Order is a tall order in itself. This becomes quickly evident by the shear fact that they already have most of the banks, corporations, healthcare and politicians in their pockets. There are two things I must announce here, before sharing some preventative measures for warding off the New World Order. One, I am not a conspiracy theorist, or anti-Semite. I'm just a realist who believes in truth and justice and as I said earlier, there are bad apples and good in every kind of peoples. And two, I do not ever condone or promote revolution. Peaceful, strategic, non-violent alternatives, are at all times the basis of my posture and stance.

Sun Tzu once said, "The supreme art of war is to subdue the enemy without fighting". So we might consider log-jamming the marching boots of fear, terror, ill-gained profits and power with some of the following measures:

- Don't use big banks. Transfer the bulk of your money in banks to a credit union, using a bank for only minimal bill-paying.

- Stop watching major network news (CBS, ABC, NBC, and CNN). "Mind control" is an old Bolshevik trick and there are too many honest, more accurate and truthful alternatives between your T.V. and the computer. Here is just a scratch of the surface:

4th Media, Pravda, ITAR-Tass, Press TV, Xinhua News, Peter Lavell, Max Keiser, CCTV, Jim Rogers, Harry Dent, RT News, Gerald Celente, Jesse Ventura, Pepe Escobar, Russia Insider, Larry King, Tom Hartman, Sputnik News, Brother Nathanael Kapner's "Real Jew News", David Duke, Indian Muslim Observer, Paul Craig Roberts, Steve Lendman, John Pilger, Veterans Today, Rense, New Eastern Outlook, Al Bawaba News, Zero Hedge, Iran Daily, The Global Times, Juice Rap News, Lasha Darkmoon's "The Truth Seeker" and Bill Whittle.

(*Reader's note: The reader may also access all the above mentioned alternative-news contacts, already linked at the author's news blog-site "Cassone' Silk Road News", at csrn.livejournal.com)

Aside from avoiding all lame-stream propaganda networks, keep in mind that only six Zionist-controlled corporations control the majority (over 90%) of US media: AOL Time Warner, Disney, Seagram's, Viacom, GE and NewsCorp. Both Seagram's Edgar Bronfman Sr. and Jr. also heavily influence alternative media's personality Alex Jones and his "Infowars" programming. On radio I'd avoid anything associated with "Clear Channel".

- Opt for homeschooling or private schools to avoid public education

- Own your future and "stop borrowing". Pay-in-full or do without

- Don't shop at Wal-mart or consumer conglomerates

- Dine-out at non-franchised establishments

- Put maybe 20% of your savings into precious metals

- Vote out incumbents

- Consider using food cooperatives and barter

- Recommend or lend this book to a friend

- Keep healthy and maintain fitness

- Strengthen family ties and allied relations

- Make new friends with people of different cultures

- Don't be a "prepper maniac"

- Utilize cross-border healthcare

- Consider opening another checking account with Bank of India (San Francisco), Bank of China (New York), or a reputable Islamic Bank

- Invest only in BRIC nation countries through ADRs' (American Depository Receipts), or quality government bonds of this same group. In the U.S., local and State municipal bonds are good, but "beware"; the bond market is set to crash terribly, within less than 2 years of the release of this book!

- Choose good over evil

- Choose compassion over usury

The unipolar world is an imposing continuum of a hegemonic imperialism dating back to the decline of the Ottoman Empire. However, the leading nations which account for the bulk of its leadership today, the EU, Turkey, UK, Israel and U.S. are themselves in decline. Somewhere along the way their principles and agenda veered off the highway of exceptionalism and they've had two wheels running in a ditch ever since.

Let's say there is a man with a reputation of being the most conscientious person in your neighborhood. He finishes watering his back lawn, fires up the patio grill and he and the family sit down to a barbecue almost every weekend. After he wraps that up he begins raking the leaves on his front lawn and picks-up any trash along his street front. Then he ventures out and proceeds to do the same for everyone's lawn in his entire neighborhood.

No, but he doesn't stop there. He offers to give everyone in his neighborhood loans too and not only that, but he helps everyone's kids with their homework. One day he's visited by three smartly dressed men in dark sunglasses. All are armed with sleek shoulder holsters sporting a handgun with silencer in each one and a loaded Uzi hanging from each of the men's left arms.

They each introduce themselves; Mr. Mossad, Mr. Pentagon and Mr. Bilderberg. After a three hour, closed door meeting with these men, the most well respected man in your neighborhood never behaves the same again. He leaves the water running in the backyard, allows the barbecue grill to catch fire and explode and he just grabs an industrial size leaf blower off his garage wall, only clearing enough in his path so he can continue to march forward.

Suddenly he begins distributing much bigger, even more generous loans to all his neighbors, but fails to tell them of their multi-compounding interest in the fine print. He stops helping the kids do their homework, starts making it a habit to siphon everyone's gas in their cars and then one day he just decides to blow up the school with everyone in it. This is what is known as "destabilization".

The NATO alliance nations are not countries anyone cares to move to anymore. They've become so caught up in ransacking their neighbors that their own States are falling apart at the seams.

Our world today runs in tandem. The multipolar world is separating from the bondage's of falling, fading masters. You have America on the outside and Israel on the inside. The real world on the outside and the underworld on the inside.

The world's masses have grown weary of the deceitful impositions and are awakening. The air is thick with bipolar abrasion and now all its people want is their identity back, their sovereignty back, their countries back, their clean balance sheets back and the control of their homeland back in the hands of its people and not some concocted security force. Dorothy has cast the curtains aside and the Wizards are now exposed for all to see. Israel, Bilderbergs, Pentagon, Banks; the serfs have grown tired of all this duality in the conniving facades. Less and less are continuing to till the fields. They are going home for the last time and may God help the wizard who stands in their way.

The multipolar world will soon break free, in tandem from its own co-orbital configuration. The EU will slowly disperse and many will jump ship. The world will take heed to avoid an uncoupled, very lonely unipolar world like plague on a stick. No bankers, no deficits, no military contractors, no wars, no Israel-Bilderbergers, no ISIS. Just 1,000 years of peace.

"If you don't demonstrate push-back, you will lose your country".

Jean-Paul Cassone'